McKenzie Ultimate Guides

McKenzie Ultimate Guides:

89 THINGS TO DO As An Airline Employee Before You QUIT

McKenzie Ultimate Guides: 89 Things To Do As An Airline Employee Before You Quit

Thanks for purchasing this book!

Head over to http://www.passrider.com/89things-thank-you so we can keep in touch and share even more travel advice.

MUG: 89 Things to do as an Airline Employee Before You Quit
by Kerwin

Published by
MUG
Houston, TX 77052

Additional copies of this e-book can be ordered directly from MUG. Quantity discounts may be available for groups, organization and retailers. Contact by email (feedback@passrider.com) for details.

McKenzie Ultimate Guides: 89 Things To Do As An
Airline Employee Before You Quit

CONTENTS

About the Author 10
Dedication 12
I Want to Hear from You! 12
Acknowledgements 12
Copy Editor 12
Introduction 13
Chapter 1 – Things to do before you depart 14
Chapter 2 – Travel Tips 21
Chapter 3 – The Things 23

   1.   Visit an airplane graveyard 23

   2.   Take a day trip to beautiful Oahu 26

   3.   Visit somewhere different every weekend
for a month 29

   4.   Fly around the world in a weekend 30

   5.   Fly around the Southern Hemisphere..........33

   6.   Fly around the world only airlines flying the
A380 38

   7.   Fly around the world on one airline brand
(almost) 39

   8.   Take a weekend trip to see the crystal-clear
Caribbean beaches 41

   9.   Take a weekend trip to Europe 44
     Austria 45
     Belgium 47
     France 47
     Germany 51
     The Netherlands 52
     United Kingdom 56

10.　　Have breakfast or dinner overlooking
Kowloon Bay in Hong Kong (check out the
Peninsula or Sheraton hotels) 59

11.　　Go have some really cheap and good
Mexican food in Mexico 63

12.　　Visit a few of the famous vineyards around
the globe...65

13.　　Visit Seoul, South Korea 76

14.　　Marvel at some of the wonders of South
America..78
　　The European feel of Buenos Aires, Argentina....................78
　　Colonia, Uruguay...80
　　Iguacu Falls, Argentina/Brazil/Paraguay 81
　　Lima, Peru (LIM) Visit Machu Picchu 81
　　Cuzco, Peru...84
　　Montevideo, Uruguay 84
　　Rio de Janeiro, Brazil..85
　　São Paulo, Brazil...89
　　Visit the Mitad del Mundo in Quito, Ecuador 91
　　Have a bottle of Argentinean wine in Argentina..................92
　　Or a bottle of Chilean chardonnay in Chile; 92
　　how cool is this?...92
　　Visit the southernmost city in the world..............................92

15.　　View the Sydney Harbour from high atop the
Sydney Harbour Bridge in Sydney 94
　　Getting There From North America 95
　　Getting There From Europe...96
　　Getting There From Asia 97
　　Getting There From The Middle East....................................98

16.　　Be spontaneous 100

17.　　Do you like horse racing and fashionable
hats? Then check out the Triple Crown horse-
racing events..102
　　Kentucky Derby 103

The Preakness Stakes 104
Belmont Stakes 105

18.   If you are a tennis fan, watch the four major
tennis opens; even if you are not, it is an excuse to
visit these fine cities 106
The Australian Tennis Open in Melbourne, ...106
Australia (MEL) 106
North America..107
The French Tennis Open at Roland Garros in Paris (CDG,
ORY)..112
Wimbledon in London (LCY, LGW, LHR,...............113
LTN, SEN, STN) 113
The U.S. Open in Flushing Meadows, Queens, New York
(LGA, JFK, ISP, EWR, HPN) 115

19.   Visit Alaska...117

20.   Visit The People's Republic of China..........120

21.   Visit Greenland 123

22.   Visit Iceland 124

23.   Visit India...130

24.   Visit Japan..135

25.   Visit Thailand 143

26.   Hike to the inside center of the Great
Pyramids of Giza 147

27.   Visit six of the seven continents, as it is a bit
difficult to get to Antarctica....................................149

28.   Visit a lock...150
Miraflores Locks, Panama...150
Ballard Locks (Hiram M. Chittenden Locks), Seattle.......152
Berlin mühlendamm schleuse Berlin..............................153
Camden Locks, London 155
Castle Lock Nottingham, United Kingdom 155

29.   Visit the Tasmanian devil in Tasmania,
Australia 157

30.   Visit the Mexican pyramids........................160

31.   Visit the Coliseum of Rome 162
32.   Visit a theme park 163
33.   Visit family and friends unexpectedly.......172
34.   Visit a U.S. national monument or memorial
that is in a city other than your own 173
35.   Watch a sports game played by your favorite
team in another city, just because you can...........176
36.   Visit a remote place 177
37.   Take the United Airlines Island Hopper...180
38.   Visit a city within one degree of the equator
       182
39.   Snorkel or scuba the Great Barrier Reef in
Australia 193
40.   Visit Petra, Jordan 195
41.   Visit all the U.S. Presidential Libraries......197
42.   Visit at least one of the world's tallest
structures...214
43.   Visit volcanoes 218
44.   Fly on the world's longest flights................220
45.   Visit the Swedish Lapland............................223
46.   Tour the headquarters of the major airplane
manufacturers..228
47.   Have a drink at the Ice Bar 233
48.   Hike to the tops of the pyramids of Tikal in
Guatemala 236
49.   Visit the 49th parallel between the U.S. and
Canada 237
50.   Fly on the world's shortest flight................239
51.   Attend a major airshow 241

52.   Spend a day watching planes land and take
off in St. Maarten (SXM) 245

53.   Spend four hours in Las Vegas just for the
heck of it 247

54.   See your favorite artist perform in a city
other than your home city 251

55.   Take your parents on a special unexpected
trip   252

56.   Decide on a Friday morning where you are
going that Friday after work and actually do it..253

57.   Go to a major international sporting event
        254

58.   Get bumped from a flight 258

59.   Fly an airline other than your own, often 259

60.   Take a trip with your co-workers 261

61.   Enjoy a beer festival or visit a brewery 264
    Anheiser-Busch Budweiser Brewery Experience..............265
    Guinness Storehouse...267
    The Heineken Experience 268

62.   Go to at least one of the annual film festivals
around the world 270

63.   Take your best friends and family on an "all
air tickets paid" trip to an international destination
        274

64.   Enter a country by air and exit by another
means of transportation or vice versa...................275

65.   Take a red-eye flight and go to work that
same day...277

66.   Go to a city and party 24 hours, then return
home   278

67.   Take a trip and do not stay in a hotel 280

68.   Do something distinctly different because
you can as an airline employee..................................282

69.   Run a marathon or similar race in any city of
your choice; especially Marathon, Greece............287

70.   Take a high-speed train 288

71.   Go see the taping of a TV show......................290

72.   Go golfing in some of the world's best golf
courses 292

73.   Climb or visit the Seven Summits................299
Mount Aconcagua in Argentina [South 300
America] 300
Mount Carstensz in Papua, Indonesia [Asia] 300
Mount Denali in Alaska, U.S. [North America] 301
Mount Elbrus in Russia [Europe]...301
Mount Everest in Nepal [Asia] 302
Mount Kilimanjaro in Tanzania [Africa]................................304
Mount Vinson in Antarctica..306

74.   Ride a camel..309

75.   Take a day trip to a North American City 311
Chicago [Midway (MDW), O'Hare (ORD)].............................311
New York City [Islip McArthur (ISP), New 312
York-JFK, LaGuardia (LGA), Newark-Liberty 312
(EWR), White Plains (HPN)] 312
Portland, Oregon (PDX) 314
San Francisco [Oakland (OAK), San Francisco...................315
(SFO), San Jose (SJO)]...315
Seattle (SEA) 316
Toronto (YYZ) 316

76.   Visit upwards of three countries all during
the same day 318

77.   Be in two continents in less than 10 minutes
320

78.   Go shopping in a foreign country 321

79.   Take a swamp boat tour in Louisiana........326

80.   Go to the rodeo 327

81.   Go see a theatre production in a foreign
country or city..329

82.   Go skiing somewhere cool............................332

83.   Fly to the Memphis airport (MEM) just to get
barbecue 336

84.   Spend some time at an aviation museum 337
   Berlin, Germany (TXL, SXF)...337
   Edinburgh, Scotland (EDI)..337
   Houston, Texas (HOU, IAH)..338
   London, England (LCY, LGW, LHR, LTN, SEN, STN)..........339
   New York, New York (EWR, HPN, ISP, JFK, LGA, SWF) ...339
   Paris, France (BVA, CDG, ORY).......................................340
   Portland, Oregon (PDX) 341
   San Diego, California (SAN)...341
   Seattle, Washington (SEA) 342
   Washington, D.C. Area (BWI, DCA, IAD)..........................342

85.   See how many airports you can land at or
take off from for one 24-hour period......................344

86.   Visit all of the states/provinces/counties in
your country by air 345

87.   Visit all the countries in any one continent
       346

88.   Visit every country in the world 347

89.   Visit all the commercial airports in the
world or at least in your immediate region, say
your own country, state, etc.......................................348

90.   Fly all the different commercial aircraft
types in existence 352

91.   Fly all the different airlines in the world .357

About the Author

In June 2011, I left the comforts of my airline job of 14.5 years and hit the road. I've not looked back since. I'm very passionate about ensuring that travelers like you have a great experience when traveling. It is my belief that this is only possible with knowledge of how the systems work. As such, I've created this volume with that in mind.

With 23 years of knowledge in the airline/aviation industry and holding a Master's degree in Aeronautical Sciences from Embry-Riddle Aeronautical University known as the "Harvard of the Skies" and having visited 121 countries/territories and counting plus having flown 171 airlines at the time of this writing (January 2018) and countless aircraft types, I'm well qualified.

Hop over to Facebook at https://www.facebook.com/passrider and "Like" our Community there and interact with your fellow Passriders.

Please drop me a line and if you see me traveling around, please say hello. Here are some additional resources:

- Passrider.com – http://www.Passrider.com

McKenzie Ultimate Guides: 89 Things To Do As An
Airline Employee Before You Quit

- Passrider weekly newsletter –

  http://www.passrider.com/signup

- Instagram –

  http://www.instagram.com/loyaltytravels

- Periscope – http://www.periscope.tv/loyaltytravels

- Twitter – http://www.twitter.com/Passriders

- YouTube – http://www.youtube.com/Passriders

- Instagram -

  http://www.instagram.com/unfamiliardestinations

Dedication

This volume is dedicated to my loving grandmother, Florence McKenzie nee McKnight, who passed away in December 2004, at the age of 96 years young. She made me who I am today; thanks, Mama.

I Want to Hear from You!

If you have any comments, please go to http://passrider.com/contact-us/, we want to hear from you.

Acknowledgements

Thanks to everyone who provided support and input.

Copy Editor

Thank you Avery Re (reworded@hotmail.com), you make me look good ☺.

McKenzie Ultimate Guides: 89 Things To Do As An Airline Employee Before You Quit

Introduction

As an airline employee, you have many opportunities that are not available to others. This guide will serve as a way to remind you of the cool things you can and should do.

If you are not an airline employee who does not have access to the benefits of almost-free flights, you can still purchase tickets for these adventures, so don't feel left out.

Note that the airline schedules shown were correct at the time the guide was created, are subject to change, and are sometimes seasonal. They are provided so you can have an idea of the flight times, duration, and aircraft type. Before you begin your journey, ensure you check the schedules at Passrider.com.

Now let's begin.

Chapter 1 – Things to do before you depart

a. **Get a passport** – If you don't already have one, you
should get one immediately. Check the Internet or your
local phone book, if you still have one, for information
on the closest passport agency or post office that
handles passport applications. Here are some links for
residents of:

- Australia –
  https://www.passports.gov.au/Web/index.aspx

- Canada – www.ppt.gc.ca/

- U.K. – www.passport.gov.uk

- U.S. –
  travel.state.gov/passport/passport_1738.html.

b. **Get travel insurance** – We never know what will
happen on our trips, so it's a good call to get travel
insurance. If you use select credit cards to pay for you
trip, it may be covered. Just check with your credit
card provider. Barring that though, I recommend just
buying travel insurance for the trip. Think of this as
not leaving your home without your passport for an
international trip. Head over to
www.passrider.com/travelinsurance for further details.

c. **Become a member of an airport/airline lounge –**
    This is one of the best things you could do as, if you
    travel often enough, it's totally worth it. I have an
    airline credit card (United Presidential Plus card) that
    comes with airport Club membership which works
    well most of the times. For the other times, my
    American Express Platinum card suffices.

    Here are a few things that I can do just because I have
    the airport lounge card:
    a) Take a shower;
    b) Get complimentary breakfast;
    c) Get complimentary drinks (I'm a big white wine
        drinker);
    d) Have complimentary Wi-Fi;
    e) Catch a snooze in select airports (London-
        Heathrow (LHR) and Tokyo-Narita (NRT), the
        American Express Centurion Lounges, select
        Lufthansa Senator Lounges to name a few);
    f) Get away from the hustle and the noise of the
        terminal.

There are several different programs to choose from at
airports around the world. In Europe, you usually have

to be a member of the airline's frequent flyer program in order to use most of the lounges, which sometimes rules out airline staff, while in the U.S., you can buy a membership.

You may also gain access to select lounges based on the credit cards you have, such as American Express and Diners Club. You can also get a Priority Pass membership at http://www.prioritypass.com that will give you access to several lounges around the world. It also comes as a benefit of having the American Express Platinum card membership.

d. **Learn a language other than your native language** – This will help you navigate other countries as you expand your travels. In some countries, the locals do speak English as a second language, but they just want to hear you try to speak the local language first. Then, oddly enough, they will talk to you in English from that point onwards. I suggest you learn Spanish or French for starters as these are two of the more common languages. Incidentally, there is an app called Duolingo for IOS (Apple) and Android that was voted the #1 free App for 2013. Try it.

e. **Purchase a good backpack** – This will help you get through airports easier. If you get one that easily fits in the overhead bin or under the seat in front of you, you are golden. Remember: All that stuff you think you need, you may not, so the backpack does not have to be that big. Only pack the essentials. A good time to shop is when the stores have sales for back-to-school stuff so you can get the best prices and the widest selections.

f. **Buy an umbrella** – Get one that is small and can fit in your carry-on bag easily. You really should never go on a trip without this item as you never know when you will need it. You can go to a major department store, a flea market, or on the streets of a major city and get one very cheaply. I actually bought one (Tote) from Macy's for $19.99, and it has lasted for four years now. I used to buy cheap ones for $2.99, and they just kept breaking. It's an investment; get a good one. And remember to take it with you when you are out and about. No point in having one if it's raining while you are out and it's in your hotel room.

g. **Get two good jackets** – Get a thick one for winter travel and a thinner one for spring travel and ensure

they are rain proof. Check the weather before leaving
for your destination and pack accordingly. Remember
that the seasons are flipped in the Northern and
Southern Hemispheres, so plan accordingly. You can
find some jackets online on Amazon.com at
http://amzn.to/2bPwIPu.

h. **Acquire a digital still and video camera** – You really
should not travel without a mechanism to record your
trip. The costs have come down quite a bit as the
quality has improved, so you will get a good deal.
Plus, your Android or iPhone takes really good videos
and photos. Check Amazon.com at
http://amzn.to/2bzc2Ae for some good values on still
and video cameras.

i. **Purchase a portable computer** – These can be pricey,
but shop around a bit until you find something you can
afford. Try for a Macintosh or a Windows-based PC. I
use a Mac myself. The Microsoft Surface is actually a
good one to try. My nephew uses it, and he loves it.
The beauty of having a computer is that you can
document your travels during your journey, store
pictures from your digital camera and phone, and,
most importantly, check flight loads when an Internet

café is not readily available and you have Internet access. Of course, you can use your phone to do this as well. A tip: Most McDonald's offer free Wi-Fi now as long as you give them some information at the sign-up process.

j.   **Get an adapter for your electrical items** – This is the device that plugs into the wall of the foreign country you are visiting. It then allows you to plug your electrical device into it. You need no transformer since electrical device usually has an auto-switching converter built in. Although most hotels will have one, or have a plug that will take your device, it is a good practice to have your own; at least two is a good idea: one for the computer and the other for your phone. Or just take a mini extension cord with you (ensure you have one that works outside of your own country). Check online at http://amzn.to/2bzdym8. You basically need one for each of the following regions, but if you check online, you can find one that has all the different adapters in one unit. Yeah, the world is complex:

   a)   Asia,

   b)   Australia,

   c)   Europe,

    d) North America,

    e) South Africa,

    f) United Kingdom.

Countries in South America use either adapters suitable for North America or for Europe, depending upon the country.

k. **Get your mobile smartphone unlocked** – This is imperative. I'm told that if you have 4G LTE, you are auto unlocked, but check with your mobile phone provider to ensure that the phone is unlocked. Then, when you arrive at your out-of-your-country destination, you can purchase a local SIM card at the airport or as soon as you arrive in the city.

If you have T-Mobile in the U.S., you can use your phone in select countries using your home allotment of data. You will pay for incoming calls though. Just check with your provider for details.

Bottom line is that you need to have Wi-Fi coverage when you travel so you can use things like Google Maps for directions as well as take photos and post them online for your friends at home to see. Plus, check-in for your flight, check loads, buy additional staff tickets, etc.

Chapter 2 – Travel Tips

Here are some tips to make your travels even smoother:

a. **Give advice to a fellow airline employee about what to do in a particular city you've visited** – You are the best travel ambassador there is, so share your information as it is usually invaluable to your fellow Passrider. Maybe you found an inexpensive hotel that caters to airline employees or you've figured out a way to do something that saves money in a particular country. Share it with your fellow Passriders. You can email me at feedback@passrider.com and, if appropriate, we will share it with others.

b. **Be familiar with your pass agreements** – Check with your pass bureau to ensure that you know the details of your agreements with other airlines. I advise that you get your tickets before you leave as you may not have time while on your journey even with the advent of electronic ticketing. If you must get tickets on your journey, be aware of the opening times of the local ticket offices and the rules surrounding non-revenue ticket issuance. Be prepared to wait, if necessary.

c. **Visit places when they are out of season** – Usually,
the flights are full to popular destinations during
popular times, so plan around that. This allows you to
get really good deals and actually get on the flights.
Consider visiting places after a big holiday.

d. **Be flexible** – Things change all the time as you know;
one minute the flight is open, the next it is full and
overbooked, with a ton of revenue and non-revenue
standbys all ahead of you on the list. So, if your
destination fills up, then just change the destination (if
you can). It is easy to change from going to the beach
in the Caribbean to sightseeing in Hong Kong instead.

e. **Do not hesitate to use an alternate airport** – So what
if the flights out of Newark, New Jersey (EWR), are
full? Did you check LaGuardia, New York (LGA);
Islip-McArthur, New York (ISP); John F. Kennedy
(JFK); White Plains, New York (HPN) or even
Philadelphia (PHL)? Or let's say the flights to Berlin
(TXL) are full. Why not try Hamburg, Germany
(HAM), and then take the train or bus to Berlin? It is
better to be in the same country rather than be across
the Atlantic Ocean, I would think.

Chapter 3 – The Things

Now that you are armed with the proper travel gear
and travel tools and have heeded the travel tips; here are
89 things (there are actually 91; I threw in a few extra),
that you should do as an airline employee before you quit:

1. Visit an airplane graveyard

Come on, you work for an airline, so you have to
admire airplanes to some degree. There are a few
places where airplanes go to "die" or where they are
held as they wait for an airline to acquire them. Here
are two of them:

- *The Mojave Desert, California, aircraft graveyard*
  (http://www.mojaveairport.com/) – Grab a flight to
  Los Angeles (LAX) (alternate airports are Ontario,
  California (ONT); Long Beach, California (LGB),
  Orange County, California (SNA), and as far away
  as San Diego (SAN)) and take the I-405 North to
  US 14 via Palmdale, California, to the town of
  Mojave. Follow the signs to the local airport.
  Check out Google Maps or ask directions as you

go on your journey. You will know you are close, once you pass Edwards Air Force base on the right. On the way up there, ensure that you stop in Palmdale to see one of the Lockheed SR-71 Blackbird that is stored out there. On your way to see the SR-71, have some lunch at a local diner on the same road. You will have some good country-style cooking.

There is a guy (or there used to be) at Mojave who will give you a tour at a minimal cost; this is highly recommended. If you are lucky, you may see the Boeing 747 that GE uses to test new engines and possibly one of Virgin Galactic's test machines.

- *Tucson, Arizona, USA* – On the other side of the Tucson Airport (TUS), away from the terminal, you will find a plethora of old planes. Just make a left out of the airport, go down the full length of the runway, then take a left again. The road will take you to one of the larger commercial airplane graveyards in the U.S.

If you turn right as you exit the airport, you will make it to the military planes graveyard. You can also visit the Pima Air Museum, which also houses another SR71 Blackbird as well as an old Air Force One aircraft, a Lockheed Constellation, a few bombers, and a model of Orville and Wilbur Wright's Wright Flyer.

Head out towards Phoenix (PHX), from the Tucson airport on I-10, and you will see some airplane tails on your left. This lot belongs to Evergreen and actually houses new airplanes. This is private property, so no trespassing please, but you can see the planes' tails from the highway. It is a sight to see.

2. Take a day trip to beautiful Oahu

From North America, you can arrive between noon and 2p from several U.S. hub cities; earlier if you leave from the U.S. West Coast, then take the local bus (TheBus) to Waikiki for a mere $2.50, which include a free transfer for up to two connections. The ride lasts about an hour. Check http://www.thebus.org for more details on "TheBus."

Once in Waikiki Beach, you can choose to hike the Diamond Head Crater (bring water with you) or go for a swim in the Pacific Ocean. Regardless of what you choose to do, ensure that you watch the remarkable golden shimmering sunset over the beach at Waikiki. After which, have a nice meal at any one of Waikiki's fine restaurants. Flights back to the U.S. starts to depart between 6p and midnight. There are also departures on Air Canada and WestJet to Vancouver. You will arrive in the U.S. mainland or Canada at the crack of dawn or just before 9a, ready for work the next day in most cases.

Here is a list of other activities for you as well:

- Surf the waves in Waikiki.

- Visit Pearl Harbor; the local bus will also take you
  there from the airport.

- Eat fresh pineapple straight from the plants at the
  Dole pineapple plantations. Go to
  www.doleplantation.com for details.

- Eat a Loco Moco (Hawaiian comfort dish) for
  breakfast. The Loco Moco is made of a hamburger
  patty, a fried egg, and brown gravy sitting on a bed
  of white rice.

- Visit another island. It's pretty easy to fly one of
  the local airlines to some of the other islands.
  There's Island Air, Hawaiian Airlines that flies
  between the islands. Check your airline agreements
  for details of the fares. Use www.passrider.com for
  the flight schedules, and, if you need a hotel, head
  over to www.passrider.com/hotelscombined.

- In Maui:
  - Hike the road to Hana.
  - Eat a Maui Taco.
  - View the stars from the top of Mount
    Haleakala in Maui. ("I never knew there were

that many stars in the night sky," says one

Passrider who has taken this voyage.)

- See the Lava tube flows on the Big Island of
  Hawaii.

3. Visit somewhere different every weekend for a month

Don't plan this one. Just check flight availability with your own airline or a partner airline on a Thursday or Friday and use that information to decide where to go for that weekend.

I've done some really great trips this way in my quest to visit all the countries in the world. Even if you go to the same city, you can explore different parts of that city or do different things each time you visit.

You can use the schedule on Passrider.com or the Airport Schedules (http://www.passrider.com/reservations/airport-schedules/) to see which markets are served from a particular airport to help with your decision.

4. Fly around the world in a weekend

Why? Because you can, that's why! It's
something that you've worked hard for. Time to make
it happen. The routings are easy too. Heading west will
get you the advantage of the International Date Line,
shaving about two hours off the trip.

One routing is:

- Los Angeles (LAX) to Hong Kong (HKG) on
  Cathay Pacific Airways (CX);
- Hong Kong to London-Heathrow (LHR) on Cathay
  Pacific, British Airways (BA), or Virgin Atlantic
  Airways (VS);
- London-Heathrow to Los Angeles on Air New
  Zealand (NZ), American Airlines (AA), British
  Airways, United Airlines (UA), or Virgin Atlantic
  Airways. If you use London-Gatwick (LGW) on
  Cathay Pacific after September 2016, you may also
  take Norwegian Airlines (DY) from Gatwick to
  Los Angeles.

Another:

- Paris-Charles de Gaulle (CDG) to Los Angeles on
  Air France (AF) or Air Tahiti Nui (TN)

- Los Angeles to Papeete, French Polynesia (PPT),
  on Air France (AF) or Air Tahiti Nui (TN);

- Papeete to Auckland, New Zealand (AKL), on Air
  Tahiti Nui or Air New Zealand;

- Auckland to Singapore (SIN) on Air New Zealand
  or Singapore Airlines (SQ);

- Singapore to Dubai, United Arab Emirates (DXB),
  on Emirates (EK) or Singapore Airlines. You can
  replace Dubai with Abu Dhabi (AUH) and then
  take Etihad (EY);

- Dubai to Paris-Charles de Gaulle on Air France or
  Emirates.

And east-bound:

- Dallas/Fort Worth (DFW) to Paris-Charles de
  Gaulle on American Airlines (AA);

- Paris-Charles de Gaulle to Hong Kong on Air
  France or Cathay Pacific Airways;

- Hong Kong to Taipei, Republic of Taiwan (TPE);
  on Cathay Pacific Airways, China Airlines (CI),

Cathay Dragon (KA), EVA Air (BR), or Hong
Kong Airlines (HX);

- Taipei to Los Angeles on China Airlines (CI) or
  EVA Air (BR);
- Los Angeles to Dallas/Fort Worth on American
  Airlines, Delta Airlines (DL), or United Airlines
  (UA) or Los Angeles to Dallas-Love Field (DAL)
  on Southwest Airlines (WN), Spirit Airlines (NK),
  or Virgin America (VX).

And yet another east-bound journey

- New York-JFK (JFK) to Vienna (VIE) on Austrian
  Airlines (OS). You can spend a whole day in
  Vienna;
- Vienna to Seoul, South Korea (ICN), on Korean
  Airlines (KE);
- Seoul to New York-JFK (JFK) on Asiana (OZ) or
  Korean Airlines (KE).

5. Fly around the Southern Hemisphere

A few years ago, wanting to do something different, I concocted an around-the-world itinerary, but only in the Southern Hemisphere. The leg I missed was the Papeete (PPT) to Easter Island leg as I did not time the flight properly. If you want to complete the routing, start with this leg first and work your way back since that flight has limited operating days. Here's the routing:

- Your home airport to São Paolo (GRU), unless GRU is your home;

- São Paolo to Johannesburg (JNB) on South African Airways (SA). Check out the airport hotel, the InterContinental Johannesburg O.R. Tambo Airport. You basically walk to it from the airport terminal. They do have a gym and a spa that you can use for a price plus a heated pool with a spectacular view;

- Johannesburg to Perth, Australia (PER), on South African Airways (SA). In Perth, you can go into the city and have a look around. You can stay in a

local hostel so you can get a much-needed shower
as well as some sleep;

- Perth to Sydney (SYD) on Jetstar Airways (JQ), Tiger Airways Australia (TT), Qantas (QF), or Virgin Australia (VA);

- Sydney to Auckland, New Zealand (AKL), on Air New Zealand (NZ), China Airlines (CI), Emirates (EK), Jetstar (JQ), LATAM (LA), Qantas (QF), or Virgin Australia (VA);

- Auckland to Papeete, French Polynesia (PPT), on Air New Zealand (NZ) or Air Tahiti Nui (TN);

- Papeete to Easter Island (IPC) on LATAM (LA). You have to ensure you plan this right as the flight from Papeete to Easter Island is not a daily flight; it's usually once a week. If for some reason you fail to make the connection at this point, then you can take a flight to Los Angeles (LAX) and then back to your home airport to at least complete that circle;

- Easter Island to Santiago, Chile (SCL), on LAN (LA);

- Santiago back to São Paolo on GOL (G3),
  LATAM Brazil (LA);

- São Paolo to your home airport.

  This is a great route to take some carriers you've
  not yet flown as quite a few tags are done on this
  routing. They may be different depending on when you
  travel.

  And here are some specifics with actual flights and
  times (subject to schedule changes of course):

a. Houston George Bush Intercontinental, Houston
   (IAH), to Guarulhos Governador André Franco
   Montoro International Airport, São Paulo (GRU) =
   4,918 miles / 7,914 kilometers | UA 105/763 21:30
   − 11:40 +1 Day

b. Guarulhos Governador André Franco Montoro
   International Airport, São Paulo (GRU), to
   Johannesburg International, Johannesburg (JNB) =
   4,628 miles / 7,447 kilometers | SA223/333 18:30
   − 07:20 +1 Day

c. Johannesburg International, Johannesburg (JNB),
   to Perth International, Perth (PER) = 5,169 miles /
   8,319 kilometers | SA280/343 21:05 − 12:20 +1

Day

d. Perth International, Perth (PER), to Sydney International, Sydney (SYD) = 2,039 miles / 3,281 kilometers | VA570/332 22:55 – 06:05 +1/ Day/JQ989/320 22:55 – 06:10 +1 Day/QF568/332 23:15 – 06:25 +1 Day

e. Sydney International, Sydney (SYD) to Auckland International, Auckland (AKL) = 1,343 miles / 2,162 kilometers | Various flight options.

f. Auckland International, Auckland (AKL) to Fa'a'ā International, Papeete (PPT) = 2,546 miles / 4,097 kilometers | NZ40/772 10:25 – 16:25 Mondays and Wednesdays only (this is your flight if you want to connect with the next segment)/ TN102/343 16:35 – 22:30 Sundays, Tuesdays and Thursdays only (take this one if you want to spend one night and a day in PPT)/NZ42/772 18:30 – 00:30 +1 Day Fridays only.

g. Fa'a'ā International, Papeete (PPT), to Mataveri International, Easter Island (IPC) = 2,643 miles / 4,254 kilometers | LA836/789 2:55 – 13:00 Tuesdays only.

h. Mataveri International, Easter Island (IPC), to

Arturo Merino Benitez International, Santiago (SCL) = 2,334 miles / 3,757 kilometers | LA836/787 15:05 – 21:50 Tuesdays only/LA842/789 14:55 – 21:40 Wed. to Sun. only

i. Arturo Merino Benitez International, Santiago (SCL), to Guarulhos Gov Andre Franco Montouro, São Paulo (GRU) = 1,626 miles / 2,618 kilometers | O68525/320 00:55 05:55/ JJ8029/321 4:10 – 9:05

j. Guarulhos Governador André Franco Montoro International Airport, São Paulo (GRU), to Houston George Bush Intercontinental, Houston (IAH) = 4,918 miles / 7,914 kilometers | UA104/763 23:35 – 06:00

Total Distance = 32,164 miles / 51,763 kilometers

Check with your pass bureau to ensure that you have agreements with all the carriers that will be involved. Spice it up a little, if you can. So if you can see the cities, do it. Ensure that you have the right visa (http://www.passrider.com/138-countries-at-least-you-can-visit-without-a-visa-using-your-u-s-passport/) for each of the countries you will traverse so there are no surprises.

6. Fly around the world only airlines flying the A380

At the time of this writing, there are 13 operators (http://www.airbus.com/aircraftfamilies/passengeraircr aft/a380family/whos-flying-the-a380/) (Air France (AF), Asiana (OZ), British Airways (BA), China Southern Airlines (CZ), Emirates (EK), Etihad (EY), Korean Airlines (KE), Lufthansa (LH), Malaysia Airlines (MH), Qantas (QF), Qatar (QR), Singapore Airlines (SQ), and Thai Airways (TG)). Also, Airbus has made it much easier now by creating this site to help you plan your trip at www.iflya380.com.

Here is one suggestion for a routing:

- Los Angeles (LAX) to Sydney (SYD), on Qantas (QF);
- Sydney to Singapore (SIN) on Singapore Airlines (SQ);
- Singapore to Dubai, United Arab Emirates (DXB), on Emirates (EK);
- Dubai to London-Heathrow (LHR) on Emirates (EK) or Qantas (QF);
- London to Los Angeles on British Airways (BA).

7. Fly around the world on one airline brand (almost)

When I first wrote this one, you could actually do
it, but now, since Virgin Australia no longer flies from
Australia to Hong Kong, you can no longer fly around
the world on one brand. And it will become an even
more distant memory if the proposed merger between
Alaska Airlines and Virgin America is completed.

Here is what you have to do to even get close to
this happening:

- London-Heathrow (LHR) to New York-JFK,
  Queens NY (JFK) on Virgin Atlantic Airways
  (VS);
- *New York-JFK, Queens NY (JFK) to Los Angeles
  (LAX) on Virgin America (VX). Hurry as Alaska
  Airlines has merged with Virgin America, and the
  Virgin America brand will not survive;*
- Los Angeles to Brisbane, Australia (BNE), on
  Virgin Australia (VA);
- Brisbane to Sydney (SYD) on Virgin Australia
  (VA);

- *Sydney to Hong Kong (HKG). This is the segment where this idea fails, so you'll have to do Cathay (CX) or Qantas (QF) on this one*;
- Hong Kong to London-Heathrow on Virgin Atlantic Airways (VS).

Still a fun way to do a round-the-world trip.

8. Take a weekend trip to see the crystal-clear Caribbean beaches

There are several beaches in the Caribbean that just show the powers of Mother Nature, and you have the ability to see them at the drop of a hat. Here are a few to consider:

- Immerse yourself in the glowing phosphorescent waters of Puerto Rico, such as Flamenco Beach in Culebra. Fly into SJU on all the major U.S. airlines, then take a flight or a ferry over to the island. You can find additional information at http://www.seepuertorico.com/en/destinations/culebra-and-vieques/. Culebra airport (CPX) has the following air service:
  - ○ José Aponte de la Torre, Puerto Rico (NRR) – Air Flamenco (F4)
  - ○ San Juan-Isla Grande, Puerto Rico (SIG) – Air Flamenco (F4)
  - ○ San Juan, Puerto Rico (SJU) – Cape Air (9K)
  - ○ San Juan, Puerto Rico (SJU) – Air Flamenco (F4)
  - ○ San Juan, Puerto Rico (SJU) – Vieques Air

Link (V4)

- o   Vieques, Puerto Rico (VQS) – Air Flamenco
  (F4)

- Swim in the blue waters of Barbados (BGI) or
  Jamaica (MBJ), especially in Negril, where there
  are seven miles of white-sand beaches. The major
  U.S. airlines serve both islands, so you have plenty
  of options. Do watch the loads, though. MBJ has
  more service from the U.S. than BGI (American
  (AA), Delta (DL) and JetBlue (B6)).

- For something different, see the Pitch Lake in
  Trinidad; not quite a beach, but worth seeing. You
  can't swim here, but, if you head to Maracas Bay
  Beach on the north side of the island, not too far
  from the capital Port of Spain, you can swim there.
  Trinidad's airport is in Port of Spain (POS) and is
  served from the U.S. by Caribbean Airlines (BW),
  JetBlue (B6), and United (UA).

- Head to the beaches of Tobago in Crown Point,
  which is near the airport. Caribbean Airlines
  provides service from its parent island Trinidad

(POS). The fares are cheap, so just buy a ticket as
the flights fill up at the last minute.

- Take a trip to the Bahamas Islands; start with
  Nassau/Paradise Island. You can't go wrong in the
  Bahamas at all as there are so many beautiful
  islands to choose from.
  - If you head to Harbour Island in the Bahamas,
    you will see the pink sand beach, Denmore
    Beach. It's just simply amazing. You have to
    fly into North Eleuthera (ELH) then take a
    local boat/water taxi to get there, it's worth it.
- Of course, you have to go to Mahoe Bay where
  you can hang out on the beach while you watch the
  planes land. Fly into St. Maarten (SXM), served by
  all the major U.S. carriers. Look for backup flights,
  though, as it can be tricky to fly into and out of this
  island.

9. Take a weekend trip to Europe

When I was an active airline employee, this was my favorite thing to do. It still is. I just don't do it as often as I used to, though.

It's easy. If you are in the U.S., take a flight that departs after work, and you arrive in Europe before noon the next morning. In Asia and Africa, you have the same luxury of choosing a similar schedule. If you are already in Europe, it's even easier for you to pop over to another city/country by taking a flight after work.

First find a place to stay by visiting http://www.passrider.com/a-place-to-stay/. Once you are sorted, you are ready to go.

If arriving from the U.S., Africa, or Asia, ensure that you take a shower on arrival as that revitalizes you until your sleep time later. Go out on the city that day and have fun. Head back to your hotel or the flat of a fellow Passrider and take a two-hour nap until about 8p. Do not sleep longer than the two hours suggested. Now you should be energized to see the city by night.

You may also take a nap as soon as you arrive, but only for about two hours as well.

The next day, depart for your hometown and sleep all the way back home as you will surely be a bit tired. Once you arrive home, go to sleep at your regular sleep time. If you head back to Asia or Africa, you would have to head for work as you would arrive first thing the next morning!

Here are some cool things you can do while visiting Europe:

Austria

The main airport is Vienna (VIE), (http://www.viennaairport.com/) located nine miles southeast of the city and home to Austrian Airlines (OS). Take the City Airport Train (CAT) into the city; journey time is about 16 minutes. Current cost is 12 EUR.

Here are some things you can do while in Austria:

- See an opera in Vienna.

- Visit Belvedere (http://www.belvedere.at/en)

- Visit Hofburg Palace (http://www.hofburg-wien.at/)

- Visit the Kunsthistorisches Museum (http://www.khm.at/en/)
- Visit Schönbrunn Palace. (http://www.schoenbrunn.at/)
- Visit St. Stephen's Cathedral in Vienna. (http://www.stephanskirche.at/)
- Pop over to Salzburg (SZG); Austria's fourth largest city, via train. You can find more information at http://www.salzburg.info/en/. This may involve an extra weekend day since the journey time is about 2.5 hours. But it depends on what you want to do and what time you arrive. Check train schedules at http://www.raileurope.com.au/train-tickets/journey-insights/article/vienna-salzburg. It's also a 50-minute flight using Austrian Airlines. Check schedules at http://www.passrider.com/reservations/advanced-search/.

These are just some of the many places you can visit in Vienna. Check http://www.vienna.info/en for additional information.

Belgium

The main airport is Brussels (BRU), located six miles (nine kilometers) northeast of the city and home to Brussels Airlines (SN). Take the airport train to Brussels Midi or City Center for all the action. You can find schedule information at http://www.belgianrail.be/.

Here are some things you can do in Belgium:

- Visit a small town in Belgium, say Bruges – fly into Brussels (BRU).

- Have a Belgian waffle with all the toppings.

- Eat French fries in Belgium; ensure that you get the local sauce.

- Have a different beer each time you order one in Brussels.

France

The three airports (http://www.aeroportsdeparis.fr/) in the country's largest city, Paris are: Paris-Beauvais (BVA), Paris-Charles de Gaulle (CDG), Paris-Orly (ORY). All three except Beauvais are connected via the RER. For Beauvais, you take a shuttle bus. There is

also international service to many other cities within
France, such as Marseilles and Nice, to name a few.

Paris has a number of things to do and is one of my
favorite European cities. I've only placed a few things
here for you to consider. You can find more at
http://www.lonelyplanet.com/france/paris/things-to-do.

- See the Eiffel Tower (http://www.tour-
  eiffel.fr/en.html); try to go as early as possible or
  do a night visit.

- Check http://www.passrider.com/a-place-to-stay/
  for places to stay. There is an Accor Hotel with a
  view of the Eiffel Tower.

- Visit the Arc de Triomphe (http://arc-de-
  triomphe.monuments-nationaux.fr/). From here,
  you get an excellent view of the city.

- Marvel at the exhibitions in the Louvre. It's not all
  about the Mona Lisa, but you should go see her as
  well.

- Not frequently visited is La Defense with views
  even better than that of The Arc de Triomphe
  without the crowd, so check it out by going to the
  La Défense subway stop.

- Walk down the Champs Elysees. Each time I do
  this, I'm still impressed.

- Walk along the banks of la Seine. In the summer,
  you can sit and have lunch or just watch people or
  the boats that go up and down the river.

- Have some fantastic French pastry with some wine
  from a local vineyard. Don't forget the cheeses.

- TimeOut Paris has information at
  http://www.timeout.com/paris/en/shopping/the-
  best-markets-in-paris about the Parisian markets.
  Check them out.

- Visit Bordeaux (BOD), which can be done in a
  weekend as well with a quick flight from Paris.
  Make sure you visit the vineyard at the airport.
  Yes, there is one there.

- Head south to Nice (NCE) and then take a trip over
  to Monaco and visit the famed Monte Carlo either
  by helicopter or by local bus or train. I took Heli
  Air Monaco –
  http://www.heliairmonaco.com/home.html, but just
  check with your airline to see if you have any
  agreements with any of the helicopter operators at

the Nice airport. You can find some information at
http://www.monaco-iq.com/transport about ground
transportation.

- Head down to Toulouse to take the Airbus factory
tour. Plus, the cuisine in this area is very good too.
Start at http://www.manatour.fr/?lang=en as you
do have to make an appointment.

Germany

There is lots to see in this country that can easily
be done in a weekend. Here are a few items:

- Go to the Christmas Markets in Germany. Fly into
  any major German city such as Berlin (TXL),
  Cologne (CGN), Frankfurt (FRA), or Munich
  (MUC), and you'll find no shortage of markets to
  attend. Cologne alone has seven markets.

- Ride or drive in a sports car on the Autobahn if you
  feel the need to speed. There is no posted speed
  limit.

- Visit the Mercedes Benz museum in Stuttgart
  (STR). There is a train from the main station in
  Stuttgart that goes out there. Go to
  www.mercedes-benz.com/museum for details.

- Explore Berlin. You can fly into Berlin-Tegel
  (TXL) or Berlin-Schönefeld (SXF), then take the
  bus/train into the city.

- Check out the coastal town of Hamburg (HAM) in
  the north, plus the model airport in the city called
  Miniatur Wunderland. Go to www.miniatur-
  wunderland.com for more details. Hamburg is
  also a canal city, so it's really nice to just walk

and enjoy the canals. Plus, one of the Bond
movies with Pierce Brosnan was filmed in the
city, if you are a James Bond buff. You can
actually visit the hotel that was featured in the
movie.

- Go deep in Germany to Suhl; this journey is done
  via trains. Go to http://www.bahn.com for train
  times.
- Go river surfing in the middle of Munich (MUC) at
  the Englischer Garten. This is pretty amazing.

The Netherlands

The main airport is Amsterdam Schipol, which is
located six miles southwest of the city. It's home to
KLM Royal Dutch Airlines (KL), Martinair (MP), and
Transavia (HV). Take the train directly from the
airport into Centraal Station, which is in the heart of
the city. Make sure you have Euros to buy your ticket
from the ticket desk. The journey time is about 10
minutes. If you need to stay at the airport, there is the
Sheraton and the Citizen M within a five-minute
walking distance of the airport.

Here are some things to do in Amsterdam:

- Rent a bike in Amsterdam and ride through the
  city; but find a place that rents bikes that are not
  marked with the company you rent them from.
  This way the locals won't know you are a tourist
  ☺. Although they probably will anyway.

- Have French fries at the Mannequin Pis
  (http://www.mannekenpis.nl/) on Damrak, not far
  from Centraal Station; these are some of the best
  fries in Amsterdam. Just walk straight down the
  street directly in front of Centraal station, and it
  will be on your right long before you get to Damm
  Square. There is almost always a queue, so you
  can't miss it.

- Hungry late at night, try the Febo
  (http://www.febodelekkerste.nl/), where you put
  money in a machine to get your food out.

- Visit a coffee shop in Amsterdam. Not only coffee
  is served here, just so you know.

- Visit the Red Light District in Amsterdam. Put
  your cameras away please.

- Check out Amsterdam North, the area behind Central station. It's accessible by a free ferry and is not usually visited by tourists.
- See the tulip fields just outside of the city.
- Shop at the Nine Streets (http://www.theninestreets.com/) shopping area for some of Amsterdam's best shopping. This is just one of the many shopping areas in the city.
- Take a canal tour or rent a small boat and paddle around or just find a bar that sits on the canal and watch the boats go by. Either way it's a lot of fun.
- You have to get some cheese, so check out De Kaaskamer van Amsterdam (http://www.kaaskamer.nl/).
- Visit the Vondelpark (http://www.hetvondelpark.net/), Amsterdam's equivalent to Central Park.
- Visit Rotterdam, just 30 minutes or so by train from the airport.
  - Rotterdam boasts one of the Netherlands' few commercial airports, Rotterdam The Hague (RTM), located three miles north of the city, so

you can fly in from another European city if
you prefer. It's 30 minutes from The Hague
and 20 minutes to Rotterdam by bus.

o   This city's architecture is really well done with
    lots to see and do as you walk, take the water
    taxi, take the train, or ride a bike throughout the
    city.

o   Visit the museums.

o   Tour the floating museum S.S. Rotterdam
    (http://ssrotterdam.nl/). Note, it's also a hotel.

o   Walk across the Erasmus Bridge.

o   Rotterdam has many odd statues like Kabouter
    Buttplug. Check it out; it's pretty funny. You'll
    see what I mean ☺.

o   If you ever get bored, you can go down by the
    docks and watch the large ships pass through
    the waterways. If you are lucky, you may see
    the MS Rotterdam
    (http://www.hollandamerica.com/cruise-
    vacation-onboard/Rotterdam) in port.

• Visit the World Court in The Hague

    o   The Hague is just 30 minutes from Centraal
        station, then you can take a local tram out to

the World Court. As you are that close, check
out Madurodam, which is a miniature version
of some of the Netherlands' best attractions,
including Schipol International airport.

United Kingdom

I'll only focus on London for this chapter as there
are many cities in the United Kingdom and complete
guides are written on the United Kingdom. You can fly
into London-Gatwick (LGW), London-Heathrow
(LHR), London-London City (LCY), London-Luton
(LTN), London-Stanstead (STN), or London-Southend
Airport (SEN).

Here are some things you can do in London:

- Visit any of the free museums.
- Talk a walk by Buckingham Palace – Victoria or
  Green Park tube stations.
  - o Watch the changing of the Guards at 11:30a
    (alternate days in the winter). You can do a
    visit, but you have to book it in advance. Go to
    http://www.royal.gov.uk/theroyalresidences/bu
    ckinghampalace.aspx for more details.

- Ride a double decker bus in London; this is quite easy since that's what's used for the buses in London. Go to http://tfl.gov.uk for details.

- Visit Windsor Castle – take a bus from Terminal 5 at Heathrow or a train from Central London. You will have to purchase tickets. Go to www.windsor.gov.uk for details.

- See Covent Gardens – Head to the Covent Gardens tube station on the Piccadilly Line. This is an amazing area with shops and all kinds of locals having fun and mostly entertaining you.

- Visit St. Paul's Cathedral via St. Paul's Cathedral tube station. Make sure you take the tour and go all the way to the top of the Cathedral. It's quite a walk, but the view is incredible.

- Take the Eurostar train from London to mainland Europe. You may have to do this if you cannot get out of London. Note: It's not really inexpensive.

- If you are a Harry Potter fan, check out the Harry Potter Experience from Warner Brothers Studios. It's a little trek out of the city, but worth it. Check out www.wbstudiotour.co.uk for details.

- For a free Harry Potter experience, don't forget to stop by and have someone take your picture at Platform 9 ¾ in Kings Cross Railway Station. For more information, check out https://www.harrypotterplatform934.com/pages/about-platform-934.
- If you need to book hotels in London, use our handy Guide at http://www.passrider.com/new-book-how-to-find-and-book-hotels-in-london-england/.

10. Have breakfast or dinner overlooking Kowloon Bay in Hong Kong (check out the Peninsula or Sheraton hotels)

Getting there is half the fun: Fly to Los Angeles (LAX) on a Friday night and take Cathay Pacific Airways (CX) to Hong Kong (HKG). You will arrive on Sunday morning at about 5:45a local time. Depending on the time of the year, there may be a second flight an hour later. You can shop all day and then take the 12:05a flight back to Los Angeles, which arrives at about 10:10p the previous day; which is O.K. as you want to arrive on Sunday although you left on Monday. You then head home from there either on a red-eye flight to the East Coast/middle of the U.S., and then you arrive in time for work on Monday.

You folks in Europe can do something similar as well. Head out on a late-afternoon flight on a Friday night and arrive in Hong Kong late the next afternoon. For the journey home, you leave just before or after midnight on Sunday night and arrive first thing the next morning.

In addition to breakfast or dinner, while there:

- Ride the tram in Hong Kong; also called the Ding Ding from the sound it makes.

- View the Hong Kong skyline from the Kowloon and Hong Kong Island sides.

- Head up to the Peak and see the beautiful skyline. You can take the train or you can take the hike up there. Ensure that you bring water with you as it's quite the trek. Coming down is really hard on the calves, so watch out. You'll meet some fun people as you walk and explore some great parts of the mountain during your hike.

- Go shopping in Stanley Market. This is where you can get some good deals. Go to www.hk-stanley-market.com for details.

- Visit the site where Kai Tak, one of world's most treacherous commercial airports, once stood.

- Visit Macau. You get your visa on arrival at the ferry port or the airport. Go to www.visitmacau.org for details). The journey is about 1.5 hours by ferry; the lines for Immigration are lengthy on either side, so give yourself adequate time for the journey. Tickets can be had at the departure station on Hong Kong Island or on Kowloon Island. You may also take a helicopter.

- Visit Guangzhou by train (depending on your citizenship, a visa may be required for mainland China travel). You can fly on Cathay Dragon (KA) or take the bus, but the train is a lot of fun. In 1.5 hours, you will arrive in this very populous industrial city, but it is far from what you may expect. The high-speed train costs between HKD 190-235, depending upon the class of service offered by the train you take. You can buy your ticket at the Hong Hum station near the Kowloon station. Just take the Airport Express from the airport and then take the complimentary Airport Express K1 Shuttle to the station in about 10 minutes. The scenery is fantastic as you get to see the Chinese people in their daily lives. The shopping is fantastic; I mean, you can buy almost everything in these mammoth discount stores. Plan your egress well and ensure you have enough passes on different carriers in case your first choices are full. It is a worthwhile trip, and you will get to see the Bayun International airport in all its glory.

- Ride the Star Ferry across the Hong Kong Harbour. The station leaves from Tsim Sha Tsui to Central and Wanchai; You can find fare and schedule information at http://www.starferry.com.hk/en/service.

11. Go have some really cheap and good Mexican food in Mexico

One of the great perks of working for an airline is that, well, we can travel, so it's not uncommon to head to another country to enjoy that country's culinary delights.

Here are some things to do in Mexico while enjoying its cuisine:

- Take the train tour through Mexico's Copper Canyon. It takes about four hours. Chihuahua (CUU) or Los Mochis (LMM) are the two nearest airports. CUU is served by Aeromexico (AM), American Airlines (AA), interjet (4O), United Airlines (UA), VivaAerobus (VB), and Volaris (Y4). LMM is served by Aeromar (VW), Aeromexico (AM), and Volaris (Y4). So, you have a few ways of getting to these two cities. Go to www.mexicoscoppercanyon.com for details.

- Visit the pyramids in Teotihuacán, just outside of Mexico City (MEX).

- Go to Guanajuato, the city behind the mountain,
  and also go leather shopping in Leon. You fly into
  BJX for this one.
- Visit the beaches in Acapulco (ACA), Cancun
  (CUN), Mazatlan (MZT), or Puerto Vallarta
  (PVR).
- See the Mayan ruins in Ixtapa/Zihjuatanjeo (ZIH).
- You can also visit the walled city of Tulum. Head
  to Cancun (CUN), then grab a tour bus or rent a car
  for the drive out to Tulum. You can find more
  information at www.tulum.com.

Note: If you are not a Mexican citizen, there is a
tourist departure tax that fluctuates from between 400 and
900 pesos ($20 to $65 USD), so don't spend all your
money in the bars and on souvenirs. Everyone except lap
children under the age of two pays the departure tax.

12. Visit a few of the famous vineyards around the globe

I've been fortunate to visit a number of vineyards during my travels. I love white wine, so that makes it all worth it. The wine preparation process is simply fascinating and amazing. And every vineyard owner I've met has a sense of ownership and pride.

I remember a trip to Girona, Costa Brava, in northern Spain (Catalunya) a few years ago. The twenty-something year-old owner was more than happy to show us around his "small vineyard" he said. I asked him how big his vineyard was, and he said, "all you can see," in a very modest tone. Later, his mom made us all lunch, which was even more amazing.

In Australia, a colleague and I visited the Palmyra vineyard in Tasmania, and we had a really great time. We knew nothing about vineyards in Tasmania; we just drove around until we found one that was accepting visitors. This particular one is named for the first initials of each of the family members.

One of my best experiences though has been
visiting the Douro Valley in Porto, Portugal, with its
rolling green valleys all along the river.

If you like wine, here are a few of the many
vineyards around the world:

- Argentina
  - Mendoza – This is the home of the famous
    Malbec red wine. Mendoza (MDZ) has its own
    airport, so you can fly into the Argentine
    capital of Buenos Aires (EZE) and then take a
    local flight to Mendoza. You can also fly from
    the downtown Buenos Aires airport Jorge
    Newberry (AEP) to Mendoza. Flights are also
    available from Lima, Peru (LIM), on LAN
    (LA); Santiago, Chile (SCL), on LAN (LA);
    and São Paolo (GRU) on GOL (G3). You can
    find more information about Argentine wines
    at www.winesofargentina.org.
- Australia
  - Tasmania. Fly into Hobart (HBA) after flying
    into one Australia's major cities such as
    Brisbane (BNE), Melbourne (MEL), or Sydney

(SYD). Jetstar (JQ), Tiger Air Australia (TT),
Qantas (QF), and Virgin Australia (VA) all
serve Hobart. Once in Hobart, rent a car and
drive through the wine region, stopping at
vineyards along the way. Remember to drink
responsibly or get a designated driver. You can
find more information about this area at
www.winetasmania.com.au/.

- Canada
  - The Ontario Wine Country is pretty amazing.
    Who knew? I found this out when I was the
    guest of the Toronto Tourist Board a few years
    back. You can fly into Toronto (YYZ or YTZ),
    then rent a car and head towards the Niagara
    area. You may also fly into Buffalo, New York
    (BUF), and head to the area. You can find
    details about the area at
    www.winecountryontario.ca/. There are at least
    four vineyards that are worth checking out –
    Henry of Pelham
    (http://www.henryofpelham.com/), Creekside
    Winery (https://www.creeksidewine.com/),
    Rosewood Estates Winery

(http://www.rosewoodwine.com/), and Peninsular Ridge (http://www.peninsularidge.com/). Here is some additional information I compiled on this area: www.cruisinaltitude.com/a-wine-tour-of-the-ontario-wine-country-travel-tip-tuesday/.

- o Not to be outdone, the Quebec region also has wines. It is necessary to fly into Montréal–Pierre Elliott Trudeau, Quebec (YUL), or Burlington, Vermont (BTV), rent a car and then head out to this region. You can find additional information at www.laroutedesvins.ca/en/.

- Chile – Chile has many, many vineyards as the plains of the Andes are very fertile. There are vineyards in Santiago, San Felipe, Ovalle, and Valparaiso, just to name a few. You can fly into Santiago, Chile (SCL), and explore the vineyards there using local transportation or take an additional flight on LAN to get closer to your particular vineyard. Santiago is served by:
  - o Aeromexico (AM), Air Canada (AC), Air France (AF), Alitalia (AZ), American (AA),

British Airways (BA), Copa (CM), Delta (DL),
GOL (G3), Iberia Airlines (IB), KLM (KL),
LATAM (LA), Qantas (QF), United (UA) and
then fly into the various cities or take a bus.
Start at
http://www.winesofchile.org/en/regions-and-
vineyards to get your bearings on the region
and what it has to offer.

- France
  - Bordeaux (BOD) – From the minute you arrive
    in Bordeaux, you know they are serious about
    wine. I mean, they have a vineyard at the
    airport! You can get to Bordeaux from any of
    the major European airports, so that makes it
    easy. You can find out more here
    www.bordeaux.com/us about the wines of
    Bordeaux.
  - Champagne – This is the only place where true
    champagne is made. The closest airport is
    located in Châlons-en-Champagne, France
    (XCR). Or you can just take a train from Paris
    to Châlons-en-Champagne or Reims. The
    region is located in the northeast of France.

You can find additional information at http://www.champagne.fr/en/discovering-champagne-region/tourism/champagne-wine-tours.

- Germany – While Germany is known for beer, it also produces wine; most famously Riesling. The best region is called the Moselle wine region. This area is similar to the Douro Valley region of Portugal with hills running down to the rivers Moselle, Saar and Ruwer. The area is just southwest of Frankfurt and south of Cologne and Dusseldorf. This means, you can fly into Frankfurt (FRA) or Cologne/Bonn (CGN) or Dusseldorf (DUS) and then take a train or rent a car from there. For added adventure you may fly into Luxembourg (LUX) and then drive to the region. You can find additional information at http://www.germany.travel/en/towns-cities-culture/gemuetlichkeit/wine-country/winegrowing-regions/moselle.html.

- Portugal

- o Douro Valley in Porto, Portugal (OPO). This
  area is pretty amazing when it comes to wine.
  It's also the home of port wine. You'll see
  exactly how beautiful this place is when you
  finally visit. You can fly into Lisbon, Portugal
  (LIS), from the U.S. on TAP Portugal (TP) and
  United (UA) and then take a short flight up to
  Porto. If you are already in Europe, many of
  the European airlines serve Porto from their
  hubs. This also includes the low-cost carriers.
  You can find more information about the
  Douro Valley at www.dourovalley.eu/en/.
- Spain
  - o Costa Brava – You have perhaps gone to
    Barcelona, right, but never Girona which is just
    north of Barcelona and in the Costa Brava
    Region of Spain. They do have their own
    airport-Girona (GRO) served by Ryanair (FR).
    In addition, you may also fly into Barcelona
    (BCN), then take a bus or a train to the region.
    This region has several wineries among other
    attractions. Start on the Tourist Board's Web

    site at http://en.costabrava.org/what-to-do/wine-route.

- o Salamanca Wine Region – I was doing some work with the Spain Tourist Board, and my assignment was to visit the Hacienda Zorita, a luxury wine hotel and spa, with amazing wines. To get to this area, you fly into Madrid (MAD) and then take a train or rent a car to Salamanca. This town is a college town with lots of history. Then head over to the Hacienda Zorita which is a hotel that has its own winery as well as an organic farm. This hotel is a part of the small luxury hotel of the world chain which means you can expect quality and luxury, and I was not disappointed. More information at https://www.the-haciendas.com/.

- USA
  - o Napa Valley, California – I've actually not been to this region, if you can believe that. I've tried a few times, but just have not made it a reality. Soon though. There are many things you can do from hiring someone to drive you around to taking the Wine Train. You can fly

into San Francisco (SFO); San Jose, California
(SJC); Oakland, California (OAK), or
Sacramento, California (SMF). More
information at www.napavalley.com/.

o New York – The state has several wine-
growing regions, including the Finger Lakes
Region, known for its sparkling wines
produced amidst beautiful scenery. You can
reach the Finger Lakes through Elmira Corning
Regional Airport in Horsehead, New York
(ELM), served by Allegiant (G4), American
Airlines (AA), and Delta Air Lines (DL); via
Rochester, New York (ROC), which is served
by Air Canada (AC), American Airlines (AA),
Delta Air Lines (DL), JetBlue (B6), Southwest
(WN), and United Airlines (UA); through
Syracuse, New York (SYR), served by Air
Canada (AC), American Airlines (AA), Delta
Air Lines (DL), JetBlue (B6), and United
Airlines (UA); or through Ithaca, New York,
Regional Airport (ITH), served by American
Airlines (AA), Delta Air Lines (DL), and
United Airlines (UA). For more information on

the Finger Lakes Region and other New York-
state wine-growing regions, visit
http://www.newyorkwines.org/wine-regions.

o   Portland, Oregon – I stayed with a friend here
for three months, so I had a chance to explore
two regions. The first one takes you south of
Portland towards the Evergreen Museum,
which I talk about in another chapter. This
region has plenty of vineyards to choose from.
One vineyard to visit is the Willamette Valley
Vineyards (www.wvv.com), off I-5 south. The
second vineyard is the Hood River Winery as
you head east along the Columbia River on I-
84. Give yourself plenty of time as there are a
lot of distractions along the way. Fly into
Portland, Oregon (PDX), then rent a car. If you
can't get into PDX, then try Eugene, Oregon
(EUG). You can find more information at
www.oregonwinecountry.org.

o   Texas – The state has several wine-growing
regions of which Fredericksburg, Texas, and
the Texas Hill Country are probably the most
famous. To visit Fredericksburg, fly into

Austin, Texas (AUS), and rent a car. AUS is
served by all the U.S. airlines from their hubs
and a few international airlines with service
from Frankfurt, Germany (FRA), on Condor
(DE), Guadalajara, Mexico (GDL), on Volaris
(Y4), London-Heathrow-(LHR) on British
Airways (BA), and Toronto (YYZ) on Air
Canada (AC). For more information on Texas
wine-growing regions, visit
http://txwineregions.tamu.edu/.

13. Visit Seoul, South Korea

Yes, this one is doable as well. Take Asiana (OZ), Korean Airlines (KE), Singapore Airlines (SQ), or United Airlines (UA) from San Francisco (SFO), or Asiana and Korean from Los Angeles (LAX). If you depart SFO, you arrive in Seoul-Incheon (ICN) between 2:50p and 6:40p the next day, depending on your departure time. If you depart LAX, you arrive in Seoul between 4:40a and 5:50p. So, depending on the flight you take, you have an entire day. The last flight to Los Angeles is on Asiana at 8:20p, arriving at 3:30p that same day.

From Europe, leave any one of the major European cities late in the evening and head for Seoul, arriving in the early afternoon. Or you can take a British Airways (BA) flight from London-Heathrow (LHR), leaving at 12:45p and arriving into Seoul at 7:30a, the next day. You can then leave a little after noon the next day arriving late afternoon the same day or take a red-eye flight arriving early Monday morning. If for some reason you can't get back on nonstop flights, there is another airport in Seoul called Seoul-Gimpo

(GMP), where you can get flights to other parts of Asia
[Beijing (PEK), Shanghai (SHA), Osaka, Japan (KIX),
Tokyo-Haneda (HND)] and then back to the U.S.
Same for ICN as well.

While there, you can shop, visit the Demilitarized
Zone, and, if you have a little extra time, go to Jeju
island. Plus, there's lots to sightsee in the city as well.
Check out the Visit Seoul site for more details –
www.visitseoul.net.

14. Marvel at some of the wonders of South America

Lots of you head to Europe for vacation, but South America has its own spectacular gems that are worth visiting. I love South America! At the time of this writing, I've still not visited Bolivia, Guyana, Paraguay, and Suriname. These are the more difficult countries to visit in this amazing continent.

The continent is rich in places to visit. Here are just a few to whet your appetite:

The European feel of Buenos Aires, Argentina

Fly into Ministro Pistarini International Airport, Buenos Aires, Argentina (EZE). The following airlines have service (subject to change):

- Aerolineas Argentinas (AR)
- Aeromexico (AM)
- Air Canada (AC)
- Air Europa (UX)
- Air France (AF)
- Air New Zealand (NZ)
- Alitalia (AZ)

- American Airlines (AA)
- Avianca (AV)
- British Airways (BA)
- Boliviana (OB)
- Conviasa (V0)
- Copa Airlines (CM)
- Cubana (CU)
- Delta Air Lines (DL)
- Emirates (EK)
- GOL (G3)
- Iberia (IB)
- KLM (KL)
- LATAM (LA)
- LAN Argentina (4R)
- Lufthansa (LH)
- Qatar (QR)
- Sky Airline (H2)
- TAM Mercosur (PZ)
- TAME (EQ)
- Turkish Airlines (TK)
- United Airlines (UA)

Fly into the downtown airport of Jorge Newbury (AEP); it's two kilometers north of the city. The following airlines have service (subject to change):

- Austral (AU)
- Aerolineas Argentinas (AR)
- Gol (G3)
- LATAM Argentina (4M)
- Omni Air International (OY)
- PLUNA (PU)

Once in Buenos Aires, enjoy the following:

- Samba
- Gorgeous architecture
- Local famous cemeteries, including the tomb of Evita Peron

Colonia, Uruguay

Fly into Buenos Aires, Argentina (EZE), and then take the Buquebus ferry service from the downtown harbor. You will be there in about an hour. This town is one of the hidden gems of South America.

Once there, you can either walk the area (recommended), rent a bike, rent a car, or take a taxi.

Ensure that you have some money for the departure tax
when you are returning to Buenos Aires. You will also
need your passport for this trip as you are going to a
different country.

Iguacu Falls, Argentina/Brazil/Paraguay

Fly into Cataratas Iguacu, Brazil (IGU), and then
head for the falls. You can also fly into Guarani
International, Paraguay (AGT), and do the same.

The same is true for Iguazu, Argentina (IGR). From
the Jorge Newbury (AEP) domestic airport near
downtown Buenos Aires, Argentina (EZE), you can fly
into IGR.

There is additional information about the airports at
http://www.iguazuargentina.com/.

Lima, Peru (LIM) Visit Machu Picchu

I could write an entire book about Machu Picchu.
It's one of the "neatest" places I've visited. Yeah, that
the simplest word I could find to really explain it ☺.

You have to take a flight to Cuzco, Peru (CUZ),
then take a train to Aguascalientes, Peru, then take a
local bus up to Machu Picchu. Or, if you are up to it;
hike up the mountain.

A good backup plan is to take LAN Peru (LP) to
Arequipa (AQP) and then to Lima if you can't get out
on the nonstop from Cuzco.

But first you must fly to Lima, Peru (LIM). Lima is
served by:

- Aerolineas Argentinas (AR)
- Aeromexico (AM)
- Air Canada (AC)
- Air Europa (UX)
- Air France (AF)
- American Airlines (AA)
- Avianca (AV)
- Aviones de Oriente (9V)
- BH Airlines (JA)
- British Airways (BA)
- Copa Airlines (CM)
- Delta Air Lines (DL)
- Iberia (IB)
- InterJet (4O)
- JetBlue (B6)
- KLM Royal Dutch Airlines (KL)
- LATAM (LA)

- LATAM (LP)

- LC BUSRE (W4)

- Pacific Wings (LW)

- Peruvian Airlines (P9)

- Pluna (PU)

- Spirit Airlines (NK)

- Star Peru (2I)

- Sunrise Airways S.A. (S6)

- TAM Mercosur (PZ)

- TAME (EQ)

- Tara Air (TA)

- United Airlines (UA)

Once you get to Lima, then you take a flight bound
for Cuzco. Here are the airlines serving this destination
from Lima:

- Avianca (AV)

- LAN (LA)

- LC BUSRE (W4)

- Peruvian Airlines (P9)

- Star Peru (2I)

Cuzco, Peru

This is a very sleepy town but is quite quaint. It is
the town that most everyone passes through on their
way to Machu Picchu. Typically, you would spend the
first night here acclimatizing yourself to the high
altitudes. Cuzco is 11,150'/3,399m. Some people don't
handle high altitudes very well. If you are one of those
persons, consult with your doctor before you go. If you
can handle Cuzco, you can handle Machu Picchu as
that's only 7,972'/2,430m.

Cuzco was once the capital of the Incan Empire, so
it's rich in history. If you can, plan on spending a few
days here. When I visited a few years ago, I only spent
one night, so I have to go back. You can find more
information at www.peru.travel/where-to-
go/cusco.aspx.

Montevideo, Uruguay

You can fly directly into this city or take the
Buquebus from downtown Buenos Aires, Argentina.
The airport is Carrasco International Airport in
Montevideo, Uruguay (MVD). The following airlines
have service (subject to change):

- Aerolineas Argentinas (AR)

- Air Europa (UX)

- Amaszonas (Z8)

- American Airlines (AA)

- Avianca (AV)

- Azul Brazilian (AD)

- Copa Airlines (CM)

- Fresh Air (Z7)

- GOL (G3)

- Iberia (IB)

- KLM Royal Dutch Airlines (KL)

- LATAM (LA)

- Silk Way Airlines (ZP)

- Sky Airline (H2)

Rio de Janeiro, Brazil

A visa is required for travel to Brazil for most citizens. Check with your local consulate. If you are a U.S. citizen, a visa is required before arriving in Brazil.

Fly into Rio de Janeiro-Antônio Carlos Jobim International, Rio de Janeiro (GIG). The following airlines have service (subject to change):

- Aerolineas Argentinas (AR)
- AeroMexico (AM)
- Air Canada (AC)
- Air France (AF)
- Alitalia (AZ)
- American Airlines (AA)
- Avianca (AV)
- Avianca Brazil (O6)
- Azul Brazilian Airlines (AD)
- British Airways (BA)
- Condor (DE)
- Copa Airlines (CM)
- Delta Air Lines (DL)
- Eidelweiss Air (WK)
- Emirates (EK)
- GOL (G3)
- Iberia (IB)
- KLM (KL)
- Lufthansa (LH)

- Passaredo Linhas Aéreas (2Z)

- Qantas (QF)

- Royal Air Maroc (AT)

- South African Airways (SA)

- Swiss (LX)

- TAAG Angola Airlines (DT)

- TAM Mercosur (PZ)

- TAP Portugal (TP)

- United Airlines (UA)

Fly into the domestic downtown airport of Santos
Dumont (SDU); it's just north Copacabana and Ipanema
beaches. The following airlines have service (subject to
change):

- Avianca Brazil (O6)

- Azul Brazilian Airlines (AD)

- Gol (G3)

- LATAM (LA)

- Passaredo Linhas Aéreas (2Z)

    Once you finally make it to Rio de Janeiro, there
are many things to keep you busy. Here are a few:

- Go see the Ipanema and Copacabana beaches.
    You've heard about them and seen them on TV.

Now go experience them for yourselves. Be vigilant when on these beaches and only take what you need with you to ensure you have a pleasant stay.

- Visit the Christ the Redeemer statue. Grab a cab and head up to the Corcovado hilltop. You can also take the Corcovado train. I've not done it using the train as yet. Perhaps on my next visit. It's quite beautiful from up there you can see all of Rio, the beaches, the ocean, and the harbor. It's like you want to stay forever. The local name is Cristo Redentor. You can find more information at www.visitbrasil.com/en/atracoes/cristo-redentor/

- Ride the Sugar Loaf Mountain (Pão de Açúcar) cable car. This is the first cable car ever installed in Brazil, and it still works today. In all my trips to Rio, I've not made it up there as yet. You can take a bus, walk, or take the subway to make your way to the first stop on the cable car. The view is supposed to be amazing, I'm told. You can find additional information at

www.visitbrasil.com/en/atracoes/pao-de-acucar/.

- Have more beef than you can eat in a lifetime
  when you visit one of the local restaurants. Be
  sure to flip the indicator once you've had enough.
  On a visit, we had no idea how it all worked and
  wondered why they would not stop bringing us
  meat ☺.

São Paulo, Brazil

This is the financial capital of South America and
Brazil. It is very different than Rio as it's very
commercial and does not have the party atmosphere of
Rio.

Fly into Guarulhos International Airport in São
Paulo (GRU). The following airlines have service
(subject to change):

- Aerolineas Argentinas (AR)
- AeroMexico (AM)
- Air Canada (AC)
- Air China (CA)
- Air Europa (UX)
- Air France (AF)

- Alitalia (AZ)

- American Airlines (AA)

- Avianca (AV)

- Avianca Brazil (O6)

- Azul Brazilian Airlines (AD)

- British Airways (BA)

- Boliviana (OB)

- Copa Airlines (CM)

- Delta Air Lines (DL)

- Etihad Airways (EY)

- Emirates (EK)

- Ethiopian Airlines (ET)

- GOL (G3)

- Iberia (IB)

- KLM (KL)

- Korean Air (KE)

- LATAM (LA)

- Lufthansa (LH)

- Passaredo Linhas Aéreas (2Z)

- Qatar (QR)

- Royal Air Maroc (AT)

- Singapore Airlines (SQ)

- South African Airways (SA)

- Swiss Airlines (LX)

- TAAG Angola Airlines (DT)

- TAM Mercosur (PZ)

- TAP Portugal (TP)

- Turkish Airlines (TK)

- United Airlines (UA)

Fly into the Congonhas domestic airport in São Paulo (CGH). The following airlines have service (subject to change):

- Avianca Brazil (O6)

- Azul Brazilian Airlines (AD)

- Gol (G3)

- Tap Portugal (TP)

The shopping in downtown São Paulo is absolutely fantastic, as are the local parks.

Visit the Mitad del Mundo in Quito, Ecuador

Fly into Quito, Ecuador (UIO), and stay for cheap at the Marriott hotel downtown. You can then rent a car which will take you to the "equator (Le Mitad del Mundo)." There is also another museum not far away

called Intinan Solar Museum, you should check it out
as well.

While in Quito, visit the El Panecillo, the Virgin
monument near downtown Quito.

Have a bottle of Argentinean wine in Argentina

I hear the Malbec from Argentina is a fine wine.
I've had it and totally agree. You can even fly into the
home of the Malbec grapes, Mendoza (MDZ), on Lan
Argentina (LA) from the Jorge Newberry Airport
(AEP). Just check your interline agreements.

Or a bottle of Chilean chardonnay in Chile; how cool is this?

No going to the corner liquor store to get that
bottle. Your friends will be impressed when you bring
them back a bottle or two as well. You may even get
some local vineyard that is only sold within the
country; what a coup! You will have to check your
luggage with the bottles carefully wrapped though.

Visit the southernmost city in the world

Depending on how you look at this, its Punta
Arenas, Chile (PUQ), or Ushuaia, Argentina (USH).

You see, Ushuaia is not connected to the mainland of
the continent, so technically Punta Arenas is the
southernmost city.

When I visited Punta Arenas a few years back, I
was given a certificate denoting the "southernmost
city." I wonder what I'll get when I visit Ushuaia?

Punta Arenas is served by BH Airlines (JA),
LATAM Airlines (LA) and Sky Airline (H2) from
Santiago, Chile (SCL) and Ushuaia is served by
Aerolineas Argentinas (AR) and LATAM Argentina
(LA) from Buenos Aires-Ezezia, (EZE) and from
Buenos Aires-Jorge Newberry (AEP), the domestic
airport. Check the fares as, depending on the time of
year you go, they may have some good fares.

If you are lucky, you may get on a flight that
makes an intermediate stop in one of the local airports.
This is always very interesting. I had stopped in
Temuco, Chile, because of a diversion due to weather
and that added to the experience in addition to adding
a new airport to my count. Puerto Montt, Chile (PMC),
was a scheduled stop at the time on the flight from
Santiago.

15. View the Sydney Harbour from high atop the Sydney Harbour Bridge in Sydney

Yes, you can do this. I've not done this just yet as I never have enough time, and it's not really my thing to dangle off the side of a structure ☺. But it does look cool. Go to www.bridgeclimb.com for more details.

Now one thing to note is that you can actually just walk across the bridge, and it's free to do so. I've done that and absolutely loved it. But if you're a little more adventurous and want to spend a little more money, you can do the dangle bit.

There are several ways to get to Sydney from around the world. And, if you are pressed for time, you can actually do it in a weekend as well. One thing to remember is that Australia requires a visa for most non-Australian citizens. Called an Electronic Travel Authority (ETA), the visa is electronic and is done online. It is also immediate, so, if you forget, you can get it all done at the last minute as long as there are no issues. If you've forgotten, the airline can do it at check-in, and then you just pay them the cost of about $20 USD. You can find out if you need one or apply

for one at https://www.eta.immi.gov.au/ETAS3/etas.
Here are some options to get there from different parts
of the world:

Getting There From North America

On a Friday, fly to Los Angeles (LAX) or San
Francisco (SFO), and then take American Airlines
(AA), Delta Air Lines (DL), Qantas Airways (QF),
United Airlines (UA), or Virgin Australia (VA) to
Sydney (SYD), arriving after nearly 15 hours on
Sunday morning at 6:20a to 7:10a. You can then head
into the city, climb the bridge, shop, and sightsee for a
bit and then head back the next day. Note that these
flight times may be seasonal, so use
www.passrider.com to check the current schedules.
Sweet huh?

There is also Air Canada (AC) using a Boeing 787-
9 (789) from Vancouver British Colombia, Canada
(YVR), and Hawaiian Airlines (HA), Jetstar (JQ), and
Qantas from Honolulu (HNL). There's also Qantas'
Airbus A380 from Dallas/Ft. Worth (DFW) to Sydney.
And the recently added United Airlines (UA) Boeing

787-9 nonstop flight from Houston, TX (IAH). So, you
have a few choices.

Getting There From Europe

There is only connecting service either via Asia or
the Middle East. You can fly the Asian carriers serving
Europe (All Nippon Airways, Cathay Pacific, Garuda
Indonesia, Japan Airlines, Korean Airlines, Thai
Airways, Singapore Airlines) and then connect via
their Asian hubs as well as the following European
carriers to the applicable Asian hubs below, then
connect to another carrier to Sydney:

- Air France (AF) from Paris-Charles de Gaulle
  (CDG)
- Austrian Airlines (OS) from Vienna (VIE)
- British Airways from London-Heathrow (LHR)
- Finnair (AY) from Helsinki (HEL)
- KLM (KL) from Amsterdam (AMS)
- Lufthansa (LH) from Frankfurt (FRA) or Munich
  (MUC)
- Norwegian Air Shuttle (DY) from Oslo, Norway
  (OSL)
- SAS (SK) from Oslo, Norway (OSL)

Getting There From Asia

Service from Bangkok (BKK) is on Thai Airways
(TG), Emirates (EK), and Qantas (QF).

Late-night/red-eye flights are available from
Denpasar-Bali, Indonesia (DPS), on Garuda Indonesia
(GA), Jetstar Airways (JQ), Qantas, and Virgin
Australia (VA).

From Beijing, service is on Air China (CA).

From New Delhi (DEL), there's Air India (AI)
using the 787-8.

Guangzhou, People's Republic of China (CAN), is
served by China Southern Airlines (CZ).

From Hong Kong (HKG), there's Cathay Pacific
Airways (CX) and Qantas (QF).

Japan Airlines (JL) has service from Tokyo-Narita
(NRT). All Nippon Airways (NH) and-Qantas operates
from Tokyo-Haneda (HND).

From Kuala Lumpur (KUL), Air Asia X (D7) and
Malaysia Airlines (MH) have daily nonstop service.

From Manila, Philippines (MNL), Cebu Pacific Air
(5J), Philippine Airlines (PA), and Qantas (QF) fly.

Service from Shanghai (PVG) is on Air China
(CA), China Eastern (MU), and Qantas (QF).

While from Singapore (SIN), there is service on
British Airways (BA), Scoot (TZ) on a 789, Singapore
Airlines (SQ), and Qantas (QF).

There is also service from Seoul, South Korea
(ICN), on Asiana (OZ) and Korean Airlines (KE).

Taipei, Taiwan (TPE), has service on China
Airlines (CI).

Getting There From The Middle East

From the Middle East, Emirates (EK) and Qantas
(QF) both have nonstop A380 service from Dubai,
United Arab Emirates (DXB) while Etihad Airways
(EY) and Virgin Australia (VA) has nonstop service
from Abu Dhabi (AUH) and Qatar from Doha (DOH).

Just check your airline's agreements and get an
itinerary that works for you. Remember to use the
schedule program at www.passrider.com to help you
plan your trip. If you have any questions, feel free to
drop me a line at feedback@passrider.com.

While in Sydney (remember they drive on the left,
so pay attention if you drive on the other side of the
road in your country), here are a few things to do as
time permits:

- Visit the Sydney Opera House;

- See the Olympic sights by taking the train out to Olympic Park;

- Do a walking tour of beautiful Sydney;

- Hug an Aussie; the people of Australia are among the friendliest I've met in my travels;

- Take a ferry from the Sydney Harbour to one of the neighboring islands; e.g. Manly (http://www.unfamiliardestinations.com/northheadsanctuarynswaustralia/);

- Take the train out to the suburbs and enjoy life outside of the big city;

- Visit the Sydney Tower;

- Visit the Blue Mountains. You can go via train from the city. You can see more details at www.bluemts.com.au/;

- Visit Hyde Park and walk down the famous Oxford Street;

- Be sure to visit St. Mary's Cathedral. More details at www.stmaryscathedral.org.au;

- And I always have a Victoria Bitters. If you are on Qantas, they actually have them onboard.

16. Be spontaneous

One of the benefits of being an airline employee is
that we can conjure up an adventure at the last
moment. Sadly, many of us don't though; often, we
just plan and plan months in advance. Not sure why
since the flights may be full anyway, and we may have
to change our plans. I understand that sometimes
planning is necessary, but we fly standby, so that
makes it a moot point at times.

Remember, you have the ability to change your
plans up to the very last second, so do it.

Here are some things to do that are truly
spontaneous, although just the fact of writing about
them makes them not, but I have to give you ideas
somehow, right?

- Go to the airport, look on the flight information
  display, pick a destination where you have not
  been, and fly there.
- Even better, walk the gates and if you see an
  aircraft type or livery that you've never flown,
  check the loads and get on it.

- Pick a country you've never visited and go there. Caution, this may not be too spontaneous if you require a visa. But as an airline employee, you should be prepared for the unexpected, so you should have a few visas under your belt such as the following:
  - Australia, you can apply online or at the check-in counter
  - Brazil, you can apply online usually take about 72 hours
  - People's Republic of China (can be had same day, if you have a consulate near you)
  - India (can be had same day but usually takes about three days)
  - Russia
  - Turkey, you can apply online

That's it for this chapter, go out there and be spontaneous! I guarantee it's a ton of fun.

17. Do you like horse racing and fashionable hats? Then check out the Triple Crown horse-racing events

My dad loves horse racing and, at some point, we'll complete the Triple Crown. For those not in the know this is the three major horse races in the United States each year (The Kentucky Derby, The Preakness Stakes, and the Belmont Stakes).

My dad and I have been to the Preakness Stakes in Baltimore, and it was a lot of fun. We flew in the night before, stayed at a hotel near the airport, took the hotel's shuttle to the airport, and then took the train and a provided shuttle bus to the track. I think we will try to get to Louisville or New York for the other two very soon.

If you are a horse-racing fan, this experience allows you to see the behind-the-scenes of one of the premier sporting events in the world. Depending on the kind of ticket you buy, you can be on the infield with all the activities going on or in the stands just sitting back and watching it all.

Like any event stadium, there are gift shops, food courts, and lots of drinks, alcoholic and non-alcoholic alike. We even got a chance to see the horses and jockeys up close before they go on the track for their races.

Also, the horse races are all about the hats worn by the ladies, so it's fun to see the different styles and colors as you walk through the stands.

One thing that stood out at the Preakness is that, after the event, the people who live right outside the track rents out their toilets so people can take a pee on their way back to the buses. It's quite a long walk, and sometimes there is quite a wait to get the buses.

Here's how to accomplish this one if you are a horse-racing fan or just want to do a major sporting event:

Kentucky Derby

This one is the first in the series and usually occurs around the first weekend in May. It's held at Churchill Downs in Louisville, Kentucky. The closest airport is Louisville (SDF). Alternate airports are: Cincinnati (CVG), Evansville, Indiana (EVV), and Lexington,

Kentucky (LEX). Indianapolis (IND), is a stretch if
you can't make it in and out and really want to go.
Most of these airports are served by the major U.S.
carriers, but the airplanes may be regional jets holding
anywhere from 37 to 76 passengers. Head over to
www.kentuckyderby.com for more details.

The Preakness Stakes

The second race is the Preakness Stakes, held in the
suburbs of Baltimore. You can fly into Baltimore
(BWI), Washington-Reagan (DCA), or Washington-
Dulles (IAD). You'll have to rent a car if you fly into
DCA or IAD. This is the one I attended with my dad.

We flew into Washington-Dulles as the flights to
the other two airports were all full, then rented a car,
and drove to the Baltimore airport, where we spent the
night at an Embassy Suites, I believe.

The next morning, we took the shuttle to the airport,
where we took the train into the city, exiting at a station
close to the track. From there, they had regular
scheduled buses. It was very well organized and, all in
all, a very nice day.

On the way back, we could have stopped in Baltimore to explore the city. However, my dad was tired so we skipped that adventure.

Belmont Stakes

You'll journey to Belmont Park in Queens, New York, to see the last race in the series (www.belmontstakes.com). You can fly into Islip McArthur (ISP), John F. Kennedy (JFK), LaGuardia (LGA), Newark-Liberty (EWR), or White Plains (HPN), then, you can rent a car. There isn't a NYC subway stop close to the race track, but there are buses, and the Long Island Railroad (LIRR) does have a stop there appropriately called "Belmont."

18. If you are a tennis fan, watch the four major tennis opens; even if you are not, it is an excuse to visit these fine cities

I was fortunate enough to see all four events in one year. It was so much fun. I felt like I too was doing the Grand Slam, as it's called.

Here's a list of the events and how to go about attempting to do the same. Even if you just go to one of them, I promise it will be worth it.

The Australian Tennis Open in Melbourne, Australia (MEL)

The event is usually held for two weeks in January at the Rod Laver Arena (www.rodlaverarena.com.au) just on the edge of the city of Melbourne, it's the grand slam that I enjoyed the most. I think it's because it was so laid back. It's also the first place and time I saw Serena and Venus Williams play in person. I had great seats, so I got a good view of the games they played.

If you live in North America, Australia is quite far away. Actually, it's quite far away from most places. Also, remember that Australia requires a visa for most non-Australian citizens. Called an Electronic Travel

Authority (ETA), the visa is electronic and is done online. It's immediate, so if you forget you can get it all done at the last minute as long as there are no issues. You can find out if you need one and/or apply for one at https://www.eta.immi.gov.au/ETAS3/etas.

You can buy tickets for the game online or when you get there as they are usually not sold out. Also, people are always getting rid of their tickets, oftentimes at face value, just outside the stadium. Watch a day or two of tennis and then return home. I'll tell you, the Aussies are very friendly, so you'll have a great time. Here's how to get to Melbourne from around the globe:

North America

From the U.S., you can fly nonstop from Los Angeles (LAX) on United (UA) and Qantas (QF) on a Boeing 787-9 and the Airbus A380 respectively. You may also do connecting service from Los Angeles (LAX) on American Airlines (AA), Delta Air Lines (DL), Qantas Airways (QF), United Airlines (UA), or Virgin Australia (VA) to Sydney (SYD) then connect to Melbourne using JetStar (JQ), Tiger Airways (TT),

Qantas (QF), or Virgin Australia (VA). In addition,
there's Qantas' Airbus A380 from Dallas/Ft. Worth
(DFW) to Sydney.

There is no nonstop service to Melbourne from
Canada and Hawaii; however, Air Canada (AC) uses a
Being 787-9 (789) and Qantas a Boeing 747-400 (744)
from Vancouver, British Colombia, Canada (YVR)
and Hawaiian Airlines (HA), Jetstar (JQ) and Qantas
from Honolulu (HNL) all fly to Sydney, then it's a
short enough flight to Melbourne.

Europe

There is only connecting service either via Asia or
the Middle East. So, you can fly the Asian carriers
serving Europe (All Nippon Airways, Cathay Pacific,
Garuda Indonesia, Japan Airlines, Korean Airlines,
Thai Airways, Singapore Airlines) and then connect
through their Asian hubs or take one of the following
European carriers to the applicable Asian hubs below,
then connect to another carrier to Sydney or
Melbourne:

- Air France (AF) from Paris-Charles de Gaulle
  (CDG);

- Austrian Airlines (OS) from Vienna (VIE);

- British Airways from London-Heathrow (LHR);

- Finnair (AY) from Helsinki (HEL);

- KLM (KL) from Amsterdam (AMS);

- Lufthansa (LH) from Frankfurt (FRA) or Munich (MUC);

- Norwegian Air Shuttle (DY) from Oslo, Norway (OSL);

- SAS (SK) from Oslo, Norway (OSL).

Asia

Jetstar (JG) and Thai Airways (TG) offer nonstop service from Bangkok (BKK) to Melbourne. You can also connect-to Sydney on Thai Airways, Emirates, and Qantas.

Garuda Airways (GA), Jetstar Airways (JG), Qantas, and Virgin Australia (VA) all fly nonstop from Denpasar-Bali, Indonesia (DPS), while connecting service through Sydney is also available from the same airlines.

Air China (CA) operates a nonstop service to Melbourne from Beijing, and you may also fly to

Sydney on the same carrier, then connect to Melbourne.

From Delhi (DEL), there's Air India (AI) using the 787-8 to both Melbourne and Sydney.

China Southern Airlines (CZ) serves Guangzhou, People's Republic of China, and they also have service to Sydney.

From Hong Kong (HKG), Cathay Pacific Airways (CX) and Qantas (QF) fly to both Melbourne and Sydney.

Only JetStar serves Melbourne from Tokyo-Narita (NRT), while Japan Airlines (JL) has service from Tokyo-Narita. All Nippon Airways (NH) and Qantas operates from Tokyo-Haneda (HND) to Sydney.

From Kuala Lumpur (KUL), Air Asia X (D7), Emirates (EK), and Malaysia Airlines (MH) have daily nonstop service to Melbourne, while Air Asia X (D7) and Malaysia Airlines (MH) have daily nonstop service to Sydney.

From Manila, Philippines (MNL), Philippine Airlines (PA) has nonstop service to Melbourne while Cebu Pacific Air (5J), Philippine Airlines, and Qantas have service to Sydney.

China Eastern (MU) and Air China (CA) provide
service from Shanghai (PVG). Air China also has
service to Sydney.

Emirates, Jetstar (JQ), Scoot (TZ), Singapore
Airlines (SQ), and Qantas all provide service from
Singapore (SIN), with Scoot on a Boeing 787-9 (789).
Scoot also flies 789s to Sydney, and British Airways
(BA), Singapore Airlines (SQ), and Qantas fly from
Singapore to Sydney, as well.

There is no nonstop service from Seoul, South
Korea (ICN), but you can fly to Sydney on Asiana
(OZ) and Korean Airlines (KE)'s Airbus A380, then
connect to Melbourne.

Taipei, Taiwan (TPE), has service on China
Airlines (CI) to both Melbourne and Sydney.

Middle East

From the Middle East, Emirates (EK) and Qantas
both have nonstop A380 service from Dubai, United
Arab Emirates (DXB), to both Melbourne and Sydney,
while Etihad Airways (EY) offers nonstop service to
Melbourne from Abu Dhabi (AUH) and joins Virgin
Australia (VA) with service to Sydney.

Once you arrive in the Melbourne airport
(http://melbourneairport.com.au/to-from-the-
airport/overview.html), you can take the Skybus into
the city. The city is quite easy to navigate, and you
take the tram or the local bus or have a timely walk to
your destination.

The French Tennis Open at Roland Garros in Paris (CDG, ORY)

The event is usually held May/June. I
recommended going towards the beginning as it's
easier to get tickets, and they are cheaper too.

Although Paris is easier to get to than Melbourne
in terms of travel time, it's a lot more difficult to get
tickets. But you can go to the Roland Garros Web site
(http://www.rolandgarros.com/en_FR/index.html) and
buy afternoon tickets. Try this link –
https://tickets.rolandgarros.com/en/fft-
members/packages-and-prices/evening-visitors.
Usually they go on sale the day before for a limited
time. If all else fails, hang around the entrance and see
if anyone has extra tickets they won't be using.

You can get to Paris from all the U.S. gateways
and the European and Asian gateway airports with no
issues. There are three airports in the Paris area: Paris-
Beauvais (BVA) [Ryanair (FR)], Paris-Charles de
Gaulle (CDG) and Paris-Orly (ORY). No visa is
required for U.S. citizens. Note that accommodations
may be at a premium.

It's easy to get to the city. Just take the RER B
from CDG and the OrlyVal to the RER B from ORY.
Once in the city, you can easily get to Roland Garros
by taking the #10 Metro Line to Port d'Auteuil then
follow the signs to the stadium.

Wimbledon in London (LCY, LGW, LHR, LTN, SEN, STN)

Held at the end of June right after the Paris Open,
it ends about 14 days later.

There are several ways to get to the tournament
venue, the All England Lawn Tennis Club, in
Wimbledon, England, via public transit.

- On London Underground, take the
  westbound District Line to Southfields (then a 15
  minutes walk) or to Wimbledon (then a 20 minutes

walk). You are better off exiting at Southfields. There will be people on hand to direct you at Southfields and Wimbledon stations.

- National Rail – Wimbledon, then the 493 bus.

I don't recommend taking a car as it is too much hassle. More details can be found at http://www.wimbledon.com/en_GB/atoz/getting_here.html.

Tournament tickets are brutal to get, but you can queue outside in hopes of getting one of the tickets for the grounds. You can also check eBay for tickets. I did queue and did get a ticket for the day. It was actually not as bad as people say it is. Besides, it did not rain, so that was so much better. And it was a sunny day when I went.

They also have a ballot system, but-you have to have applied by 31 December the prior year. Details can be found at http://www.wimbledon.com/en_GB/tickets/ballot_uk.html.

The rules for the All England Lawn Tennis Club are extremely strict so please read all the details on the web site before embarking on your journey.

Getting to London is easy as almost every airline serves this major city with its six airports. Just check your pass agreements in case you have to fly on a carrier other than your own.

There is a hefty departure tax called an "Air Passenger Duty," so ensure you check on that so you won't be surprised by the bill when you receive it. If you do a connecting flight, the taxes will be significantly lower, so consider doing that. I've even taken an overnight bus to Paris or a ferry to Dublin in order to pay less taxes. In the name of science, of course, but I digress ☺.

All in all, you will have a wonderful time.

The U.S. Open in Flushing Meadows, Queens, New York (LGA, JFK, ISP, EWR, HPN)

I lived in New York for six years and never went to see a match. Go figure. To add insult to injury, I lived in Queens, which is very close to the stadium. I just never had the time back then.

When I finally went, I had such a great time that, a few years later, I got my friend from high school to go back with me, and he too had a great time. You will, too.

This is the last in the series. The matches are held
at the end of August to the mid-September for about
two weeks. Tickets are not difficult to get. Just go to
the tournament http://www.usopen.org/index.html for
details. You can get day passes or afternoon passes.
Your day passes can get you to the courts and
respective stadiums until the folks for the evening
arrive. However, you can stay on the grounds all day if
you like. You just can't go into the stadiums. But you
can still watch matches in the outer courts and enjoy
the atmosphere.

They do have a huge screen on which to see the
matches so not to worry. Plus, like all the Slams, there
are lots of activities to keep you entertained, not to
mention food.

19. Visit Alaska

If you've not made it to the state of Alaska in the U.S., it's time. There is a lot to see and do, so you will have to return a few times. I still want to get to Barrow (BRW) and Juneau (JNU), but have not gotten around to it just yet. Alaska Airlines (AS) has a flight, AS67, that goes from Seattle to Anchorage making four stops. That's the flight I'd like to take. It would be cool to just stop in each town for a day and pick up the flight the next day, as long as the loads are still good. You should really try this one:

a. Seattle (SEA) to Ketchikan (KTN)

b. Ketchikan to Sitka (SIT)

c. Sitka to Juneau

d. Juneau to Anchorage (ANC)

Here are but a few things to check out when you decide to head to Alaska:

- Hike the Harding icefields. This is in the Kenai Mountains. You can find information at www.nps.gov/kefj/blogs/Birding-The-Harding-

Icefield-Trail.htm. This is not an easy hike, but quite worth it, it seems. You start in Seward.

- Go to Denali National Park. I did this once by first heading to Anchorage, renting a car, and then taking the drive up to the park. My colleague and I at the time did not find a place to stay before we left and were lucky enough to find a place quite close to the park, having arrived about 3a in the morning. The park is well worth visiting. It's the only place I've seen a red fox. You can find more details at www.nps.gov/dena/index.htm.

- Experience the summer solstice. I love this one as it does not really get dark. It just gets to twilight, but that's it. The odd thing is that, when you are there, you can walk the streets, and it's may be 11p at night, but it looks like noon except that there's no one on the streets ☺. It's quite an experience.

- Experience the winter solstice. In contrast in the winter time, it's pretty much dark for 24 hours. I've not experienced that one as yet.

- See the Northern Lights. This was the first time I'd seen the lights in my life, and the experience was amazing. My colleague and I looked at each other, and were pretty ecstatic to see them. We asked each other, "Was that the Northern Lights?" I've since seen them in Iceland, which was quite the treat. This is a winter-time event or late October/early November timeframe.

- Go down to Seward. The best way to do this is to rent a car and take the scenic drive down. Here, you will see the magnificent harbor, and you may be lucky enough to see a few cruise ships in port. There is also a glacier in this area, so be sure and visit it.

- You may also take the train by the Alaskan Railroad. I've not done this yet, but I want to. You can find more details at www.alaskatrain.com/routes/seward-anchorage.html. This is your departure point for the Kenai Fjords as well.

20. Visit The People's Republic of China

China is vast, and, more and more, U.S. carriers are flying to cities other than Shanghai and Beijing. More Chinese carriers are flying into the U.S. and the rest of the world, as well. This gives you plenty of opportunity to try a new carrier and explore a new uncharted territory.

I once visited Guangzhou (CAN) and had such a great time, especially visiting their zoo.

More than likely, you will need a visa to make this visit. This will take a few days, so you have to do a little planning. There are many ways to get to China, as well, so you really have no excuse. If you are in North America, there are Air Canada, American Airlines, China Airlines, China Southern, Delta Air Lines, Hainan, and United Airlines. In Europe, there are Air France, Alitalia, Austrian, British Airways, KLM, Lufthansa, and Virgin Atlantic, to name a few of the major ones. Here are some things to do:

- Buy something in China that's "Made in China." Does this one need an explanation? Most things we buy outside of China say that, so it would just be funny to buy something in China that says that ☺.

- Have Chinese food in China. Always fun and I'll tell you, it tastes very different. I once had our butler at a hotel in Beijing take us to a local place. The food was really good and not expensive at all. We paid the equivalent of $8 USD for the four of us, and it included beers. I was the only one to get sick from the food, but that's a story for another time. The others were fine.

- Visit the Great Wall in Badaling (www.badalinggreatwall.com) or Mutianyu in Beijing (PEK). The best thing to do is just to talk to your concierge, they will get a taxi for you for the day to take you where you need to go. Ensure that everything you need is written down in the local language as English is not usually widely spoken by the cab drivers. Regardless of which part of the Wall you visit, it will take a lot of walking and give you amazing views and photographs.

- Visit Tiananmen Square in Beijing. Here you'll have lots of young girls come up to you as they are looking for help with English. It does get overbearing after a while, so just politely keep walking.
- Visit the Forbidden City in Beijing. On one of end of the Square lies this City. It's pretty amazing and does take quite a while to make the trek through it.
- Next door to it is a Hutong which is very interesting to walk through. It's here that one of my friends had the chance to pilot one of the rickshaws. So fun.
- Of course, check out the following cities:
  - Chengdu (CTU) – home of the pandas;
  - Guangzhou (CAN);
  - Hangzhou (HGH);
  - Shanghai (SHA, PVG);
  - Shenzen (SZX) – you can fly into Hong Kong (HKG) and then get a visa at the border and go shopping here;
  - Xian (XIY).

21. Visit Greenland

There are not many ways to get here, and the
chances that your airline has an agreement with
Greenland Air may be slim to none. So, you may have
to look for a cheap airfare or have your pass office
drop them a line requesting a pass.

For now, you'll have to go to Keflavik, Iceland
(KEF), or Copenhagen, Denmark (CPH), or Aalborg,
Denmark, in order to get an Air Greenland (GL) flight
to Nuuk, the capital. (On a side note, Air Greenland
actually has a red livery.)

Air Iceland (NY) also has flights to Nuuk from the
Reykjavik (RKV) downtown airport. You'd have to fly
into KEF, take the shuttle bus into Reykjavik, and then
get to the airport for your flight. Air Iceland also flies
into Kangerlussuaq, Greenland (SFJ).

The more I write this, the more exciting it becomes
☺. I really need to get myself to Greenland soon. You
can find more information about Greenland at
www.greenland.com.

22. Visit Iceland

Iceland is one of the travel gems that doesn't get explored by airline employees and staff as most think it's too cold and too difficult to get to. This is not true on both counts. Iceland is not as cold as its name suggests. New York City is actually colder.

There are several different ways to get to Iceland, which is home to Icelandair (FI) and the new airline WOW Air (WW). They both have flights to many destinations, and they do serve the U.S.

There are two airports, the downtown airport in Reykjavik (RKV) and the main international airport in Keflavik (KEF). Due to its runway length, only short-hop flights operate from RKV, typically within Iceland Greenland and the Faroe Islands. Even more opportunities to explore cool places.

A neat passrider way to see Iceland is to stop on your way from Europe to the U.S. by taking an early morning flight and arriving in Reykjavik in the morning after about a three-hour flight. The airport is actually in Keflavik, which is about 45 minutes from Reykjavik.

You may also leave from the U.S. on a late Icelandair flight that arrives in Reykjavik at the crack of dawn the next day. There are several flights on several airlines from the following European cities to KEF:

- Aberdeen/Dyce, Scotland (ABZ)
- Alicante, Spain (ALC)
- Amsterdam (AMS)
- Barcelona, Spain (BCN)
- Bergen, Norway (BGO)
- Berlin-Schönefeld (SXF)
- Berlin-Tegel (TXL)
- Billund, Denmark (BLL)
- Birmingham, England (BHX)
- Bremen, Germany (BRE)
- Bristol, England (BRS)
- Brussels (BRU)
- Budapest, Hungary (BUD)
- Cologne, Germany (CGN)
- Copenhagen, Denmark (CPH)
- Dusseldorf, Germany (DUS)

- Edinburgh, Scotland (EDI)

- Frankfurt, Germany (FRA)

- Geneva, Switzerland (GVA)

- Glasgow, Scotland (GLA)

- Gothenburg, Norway (GOT)

- Hamburg, Germany (HAM)

- Helsinki (HEL)

- London-Gatwick (LGW)

- London-Heathrow (LHR)

- London-Luton (LTN)

- London-Stanstead (STN)

- Lyon, France (LYS)

- Madrid (MAD)

- Manchester, England (MAN)

- Milan-Malpensa, Italy (MXP)

- Munich (MUC)

- Nice, France (NCE)

- Oslo, Norway (OSL)

- Paris-Charles de Gaulle (CDG)

- Paris-Orly (ORY)

- Riga, Latvia (RIX)

- Rome-Fiumicino (FCO)

McKenzie Ultimate Guides: 89 Things To Do As An
Airline Employee Before You Quit

- Stockholm (ARN)
- Stuttgart, Germany (STR)
- Trondheim, Norway (TRD)
- Vienna (VIE)
- Warsaw, Poland (WAW)
- Zurich (ZRH)

American Airlines, Delta Air Lines, Icelandair, United
Airlines and WOW Air fly nonstop to and from
Canada and the U.S.:

- Anchorage, Alaska (ANC)
- Baltimore (BWI)
- Boston (BOS)
- Chicago-O'Hare (ORD)
- Cleveland, OH (CLE)
- Dallas/Ft. Worth (DFW)
- Denver (DEN)
- Edmonton, Alberta, Canada (YEG)
- Halifax, Nova Scotia, Canada (YHX)
- Kansas, MO (MCI)
- Los Angeles (LAX)
- Miami (MIA)
- Minneapolis/St. Paul (MSP)

- New York-JFK (JFK)
- New York-Newark (EWR)
- Orlando, Florida (MCO)
- Philadelphia, PA (PHL)
- Pittsburgh, PA (PIT)
- Portland, Oregon (PDX)
- Seattle (SEA)
- San Francisco (SFO)
- St. Louis, MO (STL)
- Tampa/St. Petersburg, FL (TPA)
- Toronto (YYZ)
- Vancouver, British Columbia, Canada (YVR)
- Washington-Dulles (IAD)

You can make this into a day trip returning that same evening or spend the night and return the next morning or evening. Day trips are easily done from Europe as well.

Once in Keflavik, head for the main street of this tiny seafront town, take a cab to the nearby Blue Lagoon, take a dip, pop into the city of Reykjavik for lunch and a quick look around, and then catch your afternoon flight to the U.S. or to Europe.

In addition, you can leave Europe on late-night flights, spend the night on the town in Reykjavik, see some of the sights the next morning, and then continue your journey that afternoon to the U.S. or return to Europe.

If you have enough time, there are a several waterfalls and glaciers to explore. The most popular waterfall is Gullfoss. (http://www.gullfoss.org/).

You can get around by renting a car, hiring a taxi (this is costly) or taking the bus into the city of Reykjavik.

If you like, you may also use Viator to find some tours while you visit. Here is a link - https://www.partner.viator.com/en/20971/Iceland/d55-ttd.

23. Visit India

India is an amazing country. I always tell people who
have not yet visited that it is a very different country, and
it will change your thinking once you've visited. What
amazes me the most is the huge division between the very
poor and the very rich. While you do see this disparity in
other countries, it seems wider here. There's hardly any in-
betweens. Despite all this, India is pretty amazing, and you
should definitely visit.

From the U.S., only United Airlines (UA) offers
nonstop service from its Newark-Liberty, New Jersey
(EWR) hub. From Canada, you may take Air Canada
(AC). From Europe and Asia, most of the major airlines
serve the major Indian cities of Delhi (DEL) and Mumbai
(BOM), including local carriers Air India (AI) and Jet
Airways (9W). From these two cities, you can get almost
anywhere in India by car, train, or an airplane.

Naturally, you must visit the Taj Mahal in Agra. The
best way to get there is to fly into Delhi (DEL) and hire a
car for the four-hour drive or take the train, which takes
anywhere from 100 minutes on the Gatimaan Express to
more than three hours on the regular trains. Either

experience is unforgettable. Check out the train schedules
at https://indiarailinfo.com/. You can then overnight in
Agra and head back the next day. While in Agra, you
should check out the Agra Fort which is a UNESCO
World Heritage site – http://whc.unesco.org/en/list/251.

Head to south India for the beaches and ensure that
you have some of the local spicy curries in cities such as
Kerala. More information about Kerala can be found at
www.keralatourism.org/. You fly into Cochin
International Airport (COK), then drive about two hours to
Kerala. Air service is available from:

- Abu Dhabi, United Arab Emirates (AUH), on Air
  India Express (IX), Etihad Airways (EY), and Jet
  Airways (9W)
- Bangalore, India (BLR), on Air India Express, AirAsia
  India (I5), IndiGo Airlines (6E), Jet Airways (9W),
  and Spicejet (SG)
- Bangkok-Don Mueang (DMK) on Thai Asia Airways
  (FD)
- Chennai (Madras), India (MAA), on Air India (AI),
  IndiGo Airlines (6E), and Spicejet (SG)
- Colombo, Sri Lanka (CMB), on SriLankan (UL)

- Dammam, Saudi Arabia (DMM), on Air India Express
  (IX), Jet Airways (9W), Saudi Arabian Airlines (SV)

- Delhi (DEL) on Air India (AI), IndiGo Airlines (6E),
  and Spicejet (SG)

- Doha, Qatar (DOH), on Jet Airways (9W) and Qatar
  Airways (QR)

- Dubai, United Arab Emirates (DXB), on Air India
  (AI), Air India Express (IX), Emirates (EK), FlyDubai
  (FZ), IndiGo Airlines (6E), Jet Airways (9W), and
  Spicejet (SG)

- Hyderbad, India (HYD), on IndiGo Airlines (6E) and
  Spicejet (SG)

- Jeddah, Saudi Arabia (JED), on Air India (AI) and
  Saudi Arabian Airlines (SV)

- Kuala Lumpur, Malaysia (KUL), on Air Asia (AK),
  TOR Air (OD)

- Kuwait City (KWI) on Kuwait Airways (KU)

- Male, Maldives (MLE), on Spicejet (SG)

- Manama City, Bahrain (BAH), on Gulf Air (GF)

- Mumbai (Bombay), India (BOM), on Air India (AI),
  Go Air (G8), IndiGo Airlines (6E), Jet Airways (9W),

Spicejet (SG), Air India Express (IX), and Oman Air
(WY)

- Riyadh, Ar Riyad, Saudi Arabia (RUH), on Air India
  (AI) and Saudi Arabian Airlines (SV)

- Singapore (SIN) on SilkAir (MI) and Tiger Airways
  (TR)

In the north, you can visit The City Palace in Jaipur
www.royaljaipur.in, which is located south of Delhi. You
would fly into Jaipur International (JAI) for this one.

No visit to India is complete without visiting Mumbai
(BOM). This city is enormous and, like Delhi, is bustling.
The Mumbai Central Railway station is a site to behold.
There is no shortage of air transportation into Mumbai
International Airport (BOM) from all over the world with
service from almost all the major Europe and Asian hubs,
plus service from the Middle East. Air service is available
from:

- Abu Dhabi, United Arab Emirates (AUH), on Etihad
  Airways (EY)

- Ahmedabad, India (AMD), on IndiGo Airlines (6E)

- Bangalore, India (BLR), on AirAsia India (I5) and
  IndiGo Airlines (6E)

- Kolkata, India (CCU), on IndiGo Airlines (6E)

- Chennai (Madras), India (MAA), on IndiGo Airlines
  (6E)

- Delhi (DEL) on Air India (AI), IndiGo Airlines (6E),
  Jet Airways (9W), and Spicejet (SG)

- Dubai, United Arab Emirates (DXB), on Air India
  Express (IX) and Spicejet (SG)

- Hyderabad, India (HYD), on IndiGo Airlines (6E)

- Mumbai (Bombay), India (BOM), on Air India (AI),
  Go Air (G8), IndiGo Airlines (6E), and Jet Airways
  (9W)

- Muscat, Oman (MCT), on Oman Air (WY)

- Singapore (SIN) on Scoot (TZ)

Of course, there are many other things to see in India
that I could actually write a whole guide book. So head
over to www.incredibleindia.org for more details. I've also
written some posts at
http://www.unfamiliardestinations.com/?s=india; just
search for India.

24. Visit Japan

Japan is one of my favorite places to visit. When
you do, you will see why. My main reason for loving
Japan so much is its people. They are warm, friendly,
and always find someone to translate for me as soon as
I show up ☺. Plus, they always take my picture, which
is quite fun. I'm quite the celebrity in Asia, you know
☺. Well, it seems that way. But I jest.

There are several airports serving Japan, and each
city has its own charm. The country makes it easy to
visit them as it has an extensive and very efficient
high-speed train system. Of course, the cities are also
connected by air service, primarily from Japan Airlines
(JL) and ANA (NH) with Tokyo-Haneda (HND) and
Tokyo-Narita (NRT) being the two major airports in
the country's capital city. Lucky for you, Haneda is
now open to international air traffic, so you now see
the likes of American (AA), Delta (DL), and United
(UA) flying in. When you decide to visit, here are a
few things to do:

- Eat Sushi. I'm not a fan of sushi, but Japan is the
  place to have it if you are a fan. Fish is a common

staple there, and as such, there are sushi restaurants everywhere.

- Eat a Sukiyaki dinner in Tokyo. Check this page http://www.bento.com/r-jmeat.html for some choices or ask your hotel concierge.

- Take a trip to the Tokyo Tsukiji wholesale fish market. Details are at http://www.jnto.go.jp/eng/location/spot/indutour/tsukiji-market.html. It's a little difficult to find, but worth the trip. It's also changing rapidly, so go as soon as you can. As a matter of fact, they may be moving it from its current location to make room for other profitable development. This is the market that supplies most of Tokyo with fish. It's amazing to watch it all at work. If you go, ensure that you get there very early since only a select number of people can visit each day. They start to give out tickets at 5:00a. But if you don't get a ticket, you can still hang around and watch the operation; you just can't go inside to see the tuna-fish auction. I did not get a ticket, but enjoyed watching how it all works. I even got to take a photo on the little machines that carry the fish around.

- Visit the atomic bomb blast sites and museums in Hiroshima (HIJ) and Nagasaki (NGS). Both these cities have major airports and are also served by the Japanese bullet trains. I visited Hiroshima by high-speed train, and it's a very odd feeling… but highly recommended.

- Visit Mount Fuji. This is one of the Japanese icons, and, if you are into mountains or just want to see it, you will not be disappointed. I have not visited, but have flown pass it in a Boeing 787-8. Does that count? I guess not. You can find additional details at http://www.jnto.go.jp/eng/indepth/scenic/mtfuji/fuji_05.html.

- Check out Nagoya (NGO); Japan's most fashionable city, in my mind. Fly into the Chubu Centrair International Airport (http://www.centrair.jp/en/). It's cool as it's on an island as are a few of Japan's airports. Or take the bullet train.

- Take a traditional Japanese tea (http://japanese-tea-ceremony.net). Just ask your hotel for the best place to go near where you are staying.

- See the Emperor with thousands of his subjects and tourists at the Tokyo Imperial Palace (http://www.tokyo-top-guide.com/imperial_palace.html/) on January 2 and December 23 (his birthday). Get there early, though, as there are masses of people. Outside of that, you can visit just the Palace Gardens. Here are the Tokyo subway stations to use:
  o Nijubashi-mae Station: 10-minute walk
  o Tokyo Station (Marunouchi Central Exit): 15-minute walk
  o Otemachi Station (c13b Exit): five-minute walk
  o Takebashi Station (1a Exit): five-minute walk

- Visit the Shinagawa station (http://www.jreast.co.jp/e/stations/e788.html) during rush hour. There is a Starbucks that overlooks the entrance to the JR Line. Just stand on the balcony in front of the store and watch the throngs of people go to work. I'm a people

watcher, so this is fun. There's a similar place
near the new World Trade Center in New York
City that provides something similar, but
Shinagawa is much better.

- Take the Shinkansen (Japanese bullet train)
  (http://www.shinkansen.co.jp/jikoku_hyo/en/) to
  one of the cities in Japan and watch how fast you
  go as you pass the cars on the road

- Fly into Fukuoka (FUK) (http://www.fuk-ab.co.jp/)
  as it's just a funny name and airport code for a
  city. Plus, if you log airports, it's a good one.

- If you are a guy, you can experience the Japanese
  capsules, as they are for men only. They are a
  cheap way to stay in Japan. I stayed in the
  Asakusa area, which is very central. Find and
  book these hotels at
  http://www.hostelworld.com/travel-
  features/127/capsule-hotel.

- Go to the Roppongi, Minato area
  (http://www.japan-guide.com/e/e3031.html), one
  of the many night club spots of Tokyo. Just go to
  the Roppongi station. You can also visit the

Tokyo Tower (https://www.tokyotower.co.jp/),
which is in the same area. It looks like the Eiffel
Tower in Paris.

- Go to the Tokyo SkyTree Tower
  (http://www.tokyo-skytree.jp/en/), which opened
  on May 22, 2012. You can read more about my
  visit on opening day at
  (http://cruisinaltitude.com/2012/05/22/the-tallest-
  tower-in-the-world-the-tokyo-skytree-tower-had-
  its-grand-opening-today/). Take the Tobu Line to
  the Tobu SkyTree station

Here are some additional things you should know
about Tokyo:

- The Tokyo area is served by two airports; Haneda
  (HND), the downtown airport, and Narita (NRT)
  http://www.narita-airport.jp.
- The local currency is the Japanese YEN.
- The local language is Japanese.
- You can take the Narita Express from the airport to
  the city in 53 minutes for anywhere from 2,940
  YEN to 5,990 YEN, depending on the

compartment in which you travel. Purchase your ticket in the arrivals area using cash only or downstairs at the ticket office using a kiosk. Details can be found at http://www.jreast.co.jp/e/nex/index.html.

- You can take the Friendly Airport Limousine (http://www.limousinebus.co.jp/en/) from the airport to the city for 3,000 YEN. It takes you to many area hotels in the city of Tokyo in about one to one and a half hours, depending on traffic. Call the company at 03-3665-7220 the day before you leave for reservations.

- They have heated toilet seats. Almost everyone who visits Japan takes pictures of the toilet seats. They are fantastic, I must tell you! What a smart idea.

- You are required by law to fasten your seatbelt when riding the airport transfer buses into the city.

- Portable telephones are not allowed to be used on the bus and trains since they annoy others.

- Traffic drives on the left.

- There are two terminals at Tokyo-Narita: Terminal 1 and Terminal 2.
- Words to know:
  - Hello = Konichiwa
  - Thank You = Arigato
  - Goodbye = Sayonara
  - And the coolest one, You're Welcome = Dōitashimashite
- When presenting your credit or business card to anyone, use both hands.
- Tokyo is one of the most expensive cities in the world.
- The Tokyo International Airport is located at Narita (NRT). You can take a train from the airport to the city in minutes. If you stay in hotels near the airport, they will usually have a shuttle bus to the town of Narita.
- Tipping is frowned upon; don't do it
- Get a Suica card; it's a pay-as-you-go card for the trains. More details at http://www.jreast.co.jp/e/pass/suica.html.

25. Visit Thailand

I've visited Thailand a few times, and each time I make new discoveries and have a lot of fun. I've only been to Bangkok and Ayutthaya (twice) so I know that I'm only scratching the surface as this country has a lot to offer.

The national airlines are Bangkok Airways (PG), Nok Air (DD), Thai Airways (TG), and Thai Asia Airways (FD). Many of the international carriers fly into the main airport BKK – Suvarnabhumi. The other airport in this city is Don Mueang (DMK), where most of the low-cost carriers fly. So you have plenty of lift to get you into the country.

There is no nonstop service from the U.S. at the time of this writing, but with the advent of the Boeing 787 and the Airbus A350, this more than likely will change.

When you finally visit, here are a few things for you to check out:

- When you fly into Bangkok (BKK), you can take the MRT into the city. You have a few options

from these two stations and you can get
everywhere you need in Bangkok:

- o Connect with the Metropolitan Rapid Transit
  (MRT) in Makkasan; or
- o Connect with the Bangkok Mass Transit
  System (BTS) in Phaya Thai (the last stop).

- Ride a tuk tuk – It is a three-wheeled motorized
  vehicle used as a taxi and is one of the most
  inexpensive means of transportation. They are
  noisy but quite efficient to get you around the city.

- Ride a motorcycle – These are everywhere, and
  you can jump on and off them all over the city. I
  don't like motorcycles, so I don't take them. They
  are able to cut through the traffic, and, in Bangkok,
  there is a lot of traffic.

- Visit the Grand Palace in Bangkok. – There is an
  entrance fee, and you do have to dress
  appropriately, so ensure that you read all the rules
  and abide by them before you go. You can take a
  river ferry or a local bus or, of course, a tuk tuk.
  Additional information can be found at

www.tourismthailand.org/Attraction/The-Grand-
Palace--52.

- Go to the beaches of Phuket. – Phuket (HKT) has
  its own airport with an amazing amount of lift
  between Bangkok (BKK and DMK) and Phuket.
  The flights are usually full. Check the flight loads
  before you go or just buy a ticket.

- Take a river taxi in Bangkok. – These are very
  entertaining, and you really get to see the local
  Thai people. Not many tourists take them or even
  know they exist. They are extremely fast. One tip
  is not to take any bags when you take them as it's a
  little difficult to get on and off quickly if you have
  a bag.

- Visit the temples of Ayutthaya. – This region has
  the most temples in all of Thailand. You can take
  the train from Hua Lamphong station, which is the
  last stop at one end of the MRT Blue Line. Once in
  Ayutthaya, you can rent a tuk tuk or a taxi to get
  you around the city. You can also rent bicycles as
  well.

- Take the Singapore Orient Express. – If you want a bit of luxury, try taking this luxury train to Singapore. It starts at the Hua Lamphong station. You can find more information at www.belmond.com/eastern-and-oriental-express/journeys/4_198284.

- Tour Chinatown. – Many years ago, there was an influx of Chinese immigrants to Thailand. They primarily live near the Chao Phraya River. It's quite amazing to walk through this community and sample the food, culture, and religion. It's worth the walk.

- Enjoy some lemon iced tea. – I did a tour and found this place. So I won't forget how to get there and so that I can recommend it to others, I wrote a post about it at www.passrider.com/the-best-lemon-iced-tea-you-will-ever-have-can-be-found-in-bangkok-thailand/. Trust me, you will love it.

26. Hike to the inside center of the Great Pyramids of Giza

I visited Cairo with one of my colleagues years ago. We took a TWA Boeing 767-300ER. I'd always wanted to see the pyramids, and it was amazing. I also had a chance to ride a camel, which I did not like so much.

What I did not realize is that you can actually get all the way inside of the pyramid! What was even more amazing is how smooth the walls were. Given that they did not have all the fancy tools we have now, that's pretty impressive.

To make this happen, you have to head to Cairo (CAI), and then to the city of Giza to see for yourself why the pyramids are one of the original wonders of the world. Egyptair (MS) offers the only nonstop from the U.S., or you can connect via the hubs for the major European carriers. Once in Giza, you take a local cab. You will be taken to purchase papyrus and carpets as well as perfume. You are not obligated to purchase anything, but it helps if you do. It's all part of how things are in Egypt.

While in Egypt, check out the pharaohs' tombs in
the Cairo Museum. You will have to store your camera
before you go in, though. Oh yeah, cameras: You'll
have to leave them outside when you go into the
pyramid. You'll just have to trust your cab driver as no
cameras are allowed.

27. Visit six of the seven continents, as it is a bit difficult to get to Antarctica

Our world is large, but it's really quite small ☺.
It's an amazing place despite what you see on TV
sometimes. You have such a great benefit; use it to see
the world. That's why I wrote this book, so you can
see just the tip of the iceberg that's out there. So pick a
place in each of these areas and go: Africa, Asia,
Australia, Europe, North America and South America.

And if you can, why not make it to Antarctica.
Here's a few companies that head there:

- https://www.gadventures.com/destinations/polar/antarctica/
- http://www.nationalgeographicexpeditions.com/expeditions/antarctica-cruise/detail
- http://www.polarcruises.com/antarctica
- http://www.quarkexpeditions.com/en/antarctic

28. Visit a lock

There are many locks around the world that are quite unique. Locks are an intricate way to allow ships/boats to move from one waterway to another that is at a different level. It's such a beautiful thing to see, and I've had the pleasure to see a few of them around the world (Germany, Panama, the U.K., and the U.S.).

If you are in one of the locations mentioned and have seen all the place has to offer, try heading over to visit one of these man-made marvels. Some are automated, while others are completely manual. Here are but a few of them to check out:

Miraflores Locks, Panama

To reach this one, you have to fly into Panama City (PTY). This airport is the home of Copa Airlines (CM), which has an amazing network to the Caribbean, Central, North, and South America. There's even planned service by Emirates (EK) from Dubai (DXB). This will be the world's longest flight when it happens. Then there's service from Europe:

- Air France (AF)

- o Paris-Charles de Gaulle (CDG)
- Iberia (IB)
  - o Madrid (MAD)
- KLM (KL)
  - o Amsterdam (AMS)
- Lufthansa (LH)
  - o Frankfurt, Germany (FRA)
- TAP Portugal (TP)
  - o Lisbon, Portugal (LIS)

The airport is also served with nonstop service by the
following airlines from North America:

- Air Canada (AC)
  - o Toronto (YYZ)
- American (AA)
  - o Dallas/Ft. Worth (DFW)
  - o Miami (MIA)
- Delta Air Lines (DL)
  - o Atlanta (ATL)
- Spirit Airlines (NK)
  - o Fort Lauderdale, Florida (FLL)
- United (UA)

- o   Denver (DEN)

- o   Houston-Intercontinental (IAH)

- o   Newark-Liberty, New Jersey (EWR)

Watch the super tankers go through the Miraflores Locks of the Panama Canal. You will need to rent a car and drive out there though. The drive is quite scenic and allows you to see Panama as well. Ensure that you give yourself enough time so you get there before the Welcome Center closes. Even if you miss it; i.e. get there after it's closed to public tours, you can still watch the ships come through. It's fascinating.

Ballard Locks (Hiram M. Chittenden Locks), Seattle

You perhaps had no idea that this place existed, huh? To experience it, fly into Seattle (SEA) and rent a car, then head north on I-5 up to the locks. If you can't get into Seattle, then try flying into Vancouver, British Columbia, Canada (YVR), and then taking Air Canada Jazz (AC), Alaska Airlines (Horizon Airlines) (AS*), or Delta Air Lines (DL*).

You can watch the boats go through the Ballard Locks of Seattle into the Puget Sound. The surrounding is quite nice to explore, and there is also a park area to relax as well.

Depending on the time of year you are there, you will be able to see the salmon head upstream as well.

Berlin mühlendamm schleuse Berlin

Berlin does not have many nonstop services from the U.S., but has plenty from Europe to both Berlin-Tegel (TXL) and Berlin-Schönefeld (SXF). You can find additional information at http://www.wsa-b.de/wasserstrassen/schleusen/schl_muehlendamm/.

From the U.S., you can take Delta Air Lines (DL) seasonally from New York-JFK, New York NY (JFK) and United (UA) from Newark-Liberty, New Jersey (EWR). Of course, you can always connect from all the hubs of the major European carriers.

Don't forget it's Germany, so you can take a train to almost everywhere, and, of course, Berlin is no exception. You can fly to any other city in Europe and then take a train to Berlin.

Here's a tip: If you plan at least three days out, you can get much cheaper train tickets.

Plus you can take intra-Europe buses to get to
Berlin. So for example, you can fly into, say,
Hamburg, Germany (HAM), and then take a bus to
Berlin. FlixBus (http://www.flixbus.com) and Berlin
Linien Bus (https://www.berlinlinienbus.de/?lang=en)
operate buses with fares as low as eight EUR. Last-
minute fares are not bad, either, sometimes for the
same eight EUR. I've taken the FlixBus before, and
the buses are very comfortable and offer free WiFi.
Take your own refreshments, though. Most buses have
power either at every seat or every other seat. How
cool is that?

So you made it to Berlin. The dam, which is
located in the East Berlin Mitte area, dates back to the
19th century. It's located on the River Spree that runs
through the city.

The riverboats usually go up to this point in the
Spree and then turn around. You can get a look at it,
but you have to be quick. So it's worth it to take a
special trip just to see the lock ☺.

You can take the U2 (train) to Klosterstrasse, then
walk toward the river. There are also a few local buses
that will take you even closer. The area is quite

beautiful, as well, so you won't be disappointed. Soon,
you'll see the boats going through the lock. Get your
camera ready.

Camden Locks, London

Fly into London-Gatwick (LGW) or London-
Heathrow (LHR) from the U.S. or into one of the other
four airports in the London area (London-City (LCY),
London-Luton (LTN), London-Southend (SEN) and
London-Stanstead (STN)). Although this lock is no
longer functional, it is a beauty to see in addition to
visiting all the eclectic shops that are located in that
area. Take the Northern Line Underground to the
Camden Town stop. The lock is located just across
from the Camden Market.

Castle Lock Nottingham, United Kingdom

You can fly into the main London airports and then
take a train up to Nottingham. You can also fly into
Birmingham (BHX) or Manchester (MAN) if coming
from the U.S. or other European cities, then take a
train to Nottingham. The East Midlands Airport
(EMA) is also close by. Head over to

https://canalrivertrust.org.uk/places-to-visit/destination/20/nottingham-castle-wharf for more details.

Just head down into the city by the river Trent that runs through the city. The area is called the Castle Wharfs with beautiful cafes, restaurants, and the river. You will see the narrow boats going along the river throughout the city. There are a few locks, and the sailors have to operate them manually. It's a beautiful sight to see. The one in the city is Castle Lock #6.

While there, check out other things to see in Nottingham, including The Sherriff of Nottingham and Robin Hood (yes, he does exist). The city also has caves and castles and excellent pubs with good beer. So there is a lot to do.

You can find these locks all over the U.K. It's a beautiful thing to watch the narrow boats go through them. Check http://www.visitthames.co.uk/about-the-river/river-thames-locks for a list of Locks in the U.K.

29. Visit the Tasmanian devil in Tasmania, Australia

Yes, such a thing exists in real life. It's not just a character in a cartoon.

First you fly to Brisbane (BNE), Melbourne (MEL), or Sydney (SYD). From the U.S., American Airlines (AA), Delta Air Lines (DL), Hawaiian Airlines (HA), and United Airlines (UA) offer service. Qantas (QF) also provides service from the U.S. West Coast and Dallas/Ft. Worth (DFW).

Air Canada (AC) has service from Vancouver, British Columbia, Canada (YVR).

There is plenty of lift from Asia (Bangkok (BKK), Hong Kong (HKG), Singapore (SIN) and Tokyo (HND, NRT) to name a few), so you have a few options.

Once in mainland Australia, take another flight down to Hobart in Tasmania (HBA). The following airlines have service to Hobart: Jetstar (JQ), Tiger Air Australia (TT), Qantas (QF), and Virgin Australia (VA). An additional flight to look for is Jetstar (JQ)

flying out of Melbourne-Avalon Airport (AVV).
Check your pass agreements.

It is necessary to rent a car and then head for the
zoo, which is located in Launceston (1166 Ecclestone
Road Riverside, TAS 7250). It is a two to three-and-a-
half-hour drive depending on the route you take.

Remember that a visa is required for U.S. citizens.
Non-U.S. citizens should check with the consulate for
your country of citizenship to find out your
requirements. Select citizens, including from the U.S.
and Canada, can apply online for a fee for the ETA at
www.eta.immi.gov.au/ETAS3/etas. I recommended
that you get your visa online as opposed to at the
airport. Just in case there are any issues, you can
straighten them out. The visa is valid for one year with
multiple entries. More information about traveling to
Australia as a U.S. citizen can be found at
https://travel.state.gov/content/passports/en/country/au
stralia.html. In addition, IATA has created an interface
at www.iatatravelcentre.com where you can find visa
and health requirements for citizens of all countries.

Additional details can be found at www.tasmaniazoo.com.au/. Tazzy will be waiting. Caution, do not put your hand in the cage…

While there, feed and pet a kangaroo and check out a joey (a baby kangaroo).

Remember that Australia is in the southern hemisphere, so the seasons are flipped if you live in the northern hemisphere.

30. Visit the Mexican pyramids

Most people journey to Egypt to see the pyramids, but you can have an equally good experience in Mexico as well. Here are four places worth visiting where you can enjoy the Mayan civilization:

- Chichén Itzá – Yucatan Peninsula, Mexico
- Coba – You've perhaps not heard much about this place, but not far from Tulum sits Coba. It's a pretty amazing place. The closest airport is Cancun (CUN), which is served by almost all of the U.S. airlines and also some from Canada. You can walk or rent a bike. Rent the bike ☺. After a long walk or ride, you will arrive at this amazing pyramid with very precarious steps that take you to the top, giving you a wonderful view of the canopy of trees around you. You almost get a 360-degree view from up there. I did the tour with Alltournative at www.alltournative.com/. It's much easier than me figuring it all out for myself. They do other tours to cenotes as well as other Mayan ruins.
- Teotihuacán – Located just outside of Mexico City (MEX), these two pyramids called the sun and the

moon are spectacular. Aeromexico (AM), interjet, VivaAeroBus, Volaris, and the major U.S. carriers all serve the Mexico City airport, which is the closest to the attraction, so you have plenty of options. If MEX is full though, you can try Toluca (TLC) and Puebla (PBC) and then rent a car and drive in. Bring lots of water as climbing the pyramids will take some effort. Plus, the elevation of the area just adds to the experience. Here is some additional information about the pyramids – www.visitmexico.com/en/adventure-and-fun-teotihuacan. There are also a few caves around the area worth exploring. One of them even has a restaurant. It's called La Gruta Teotihuacán. More details at www.lagruta.mx.

- Tulum – Just about a half-hour drive from Coba is Tulum, the seaside Mayan town. You can find some more information about Tulum at www.visitmexico.com/en/tulum-ancient-mayan-fortress-in-riviera-maya.

31. Visit the Coliseum of Rome

It took me a few visits to Rome before I actually
visited the Coliseum, also known as the Flavian
Amphitheatre. Other than just to see it in passing. I
encourage you to take a visit the next time you are in
Rome. But don't just walk by or do it on your own.
Get a tour guide.

I went in 2015 and had a sponsored tour by Walks
of Italy (http://www.passrider.com/travel-
tools/tours/walks-of-italy-tours/). There are other tour
companies as well, but these guys are professional, and
I had quite a good time.

Fly in to Rome-Fiumicino (FCO), the home of
Alitalia (AZ), and then take the bus into the city. You
may also take the train, but it's much cheaper to take
the bus.

You can get to FCO from the U.S. on Alitalia
(AZ), American (AA), Delta (DL) and United (UA).
Plus Air Canada (AC) and Air Transat (TS) from
Montreal (YUL) and Toronto (YYZ) in Canada.

32. Visit a theme park

These are great places to just let loose and have a great time. If you plan properly, you can do these on day trips, so you save the cost of a hotel night; however, some will take a little longer and a little more planning. Here are a few to consider:

- Alton Towers, Staffordshire, England (www.altontowers.com) – Fly into Birmingham (BHX) or Manchester (MAN), then take a train to the Alton station.

- Cedar Point, Sandusky, Ohio (www.cedarpoint.com) – Fly into Toledo, Ohio (TOL), or Cleveland (CLE), then rent a car. You may also do Detroit (DTW), but the drive is longer.

- Coney Island, Brooklyn, New York (www.coneyislandpark.com) – Fly into any of the three New York City-area airports (JFK, La-Guardia (LGA) or Newark, New Jersey (EWR)), connect to the NYC Subway Q train to the Ocean Parkway stop, then walk to Coney Island. You may also rent a car and drive.

- Dollywood, Pigeon Forge, Tennessee
  (www.dollywood.com) – Fly into Knoxville,
  Tennessee (TYS), or Asheville, North Carolina
  (AVL). If those won't work, try Chattanooga,
  Tennessee (CHA), or Greenville/Spartanburg,
  South Carolina (GSP). You will need to rent a car
  regardless of the airport you choose.

- The Walt Disney Resorts are a deal – so much so
  that I have two friends who have a site and a
  podcast dedicated to it all. Check out Erin De
  Santiago's site at www.disneyglobetrotter.com and
  Lou Mongello's at www.wdwradio.com. These
  two people are the ultimate Disney experts that I
  know. Now onto the details of how to get to the
  resorts:

  o Disneyland, Anaheim, California
    (https://disneyland.disney.go.com/) – Fly into
    Orange County Airport (SNA). There are
    shuttle buses from the airport, or you can rent a
    car. You can also fly into the Los Angeles-area
    airports (BUR, LAX, LGB, and ONT) and rent
    a car to the facility.

o Hong Kong Disneyland, Lantau Island Hong Kong (www.hongkongdisneyland.com) – Fly into Hong Kong (HKG) and take ground transportation or the train from Sunny Bay station to the resort. If you are already in Hong Kong, you can take the MTR from Sunny Bay Station to the resort. No visa is required for U.S. citizens to enter Hong Kong. Check with the Hong Kong consulate in your area for visa requirements.

o Disneyland Paris, Marne-la-Vallée, France (www.disneylandparis.com) – Fly into Paris-Charles de Gaulle (CDG) or Paris-Orly (ORY) and take the Magic Shuttle airport bus (www.magicalshuttle.co.uk) to the resort. There is an additional charge for this shuttle. If you desire, you can take a local train, the RER A, to the Marne-la-Vallée/Chessy train station, which is right by the resort. There are free shuttles from this station.

o Disneyland Tokyo, Urayasu, Chiba, Japan (www.tokyodisneyresort.jp/en/tdl/) – Fly into Tokyo-Narita (NRT) or Tokyo-Haneda (HND).

From the Narita airport, you would take the JR Narita Express to Tokyo Station, then take either the Keiyo or the Musashino JR lines to Maihama station. Take the Haneda Express from Haneda. There are also shuttle buses from several of the main stations in the city of Tokyo. This page gives you several options to choose from (www.tokyodisneyresort.jp/en/access/).

o Disneyworld, Orlando, Florida (https://disneyworld.disney.go.com/) – Fly into Orlando, Florida (MCO). There is a complimentary shuttle bus, called Disney's Magical Express, from the airport to the resort if you are staying at the resort. Otherwise, you can rent a car.

o Shanghai Disney Resort, Shanghai (www.shanghaidisneyresort.com) – This is the newest park, which opened June 16, 2016. Fly into Shanghai-Pudong (PVG). Take Line 11 to the final stop of the Shanghai Metro. There are also several bus lines that will take you there as there is a transportation hub at the property.

More than likely, you will require a visa, so be sure and check that. The good thing is that U.S. citizens can now apply for a ten-year visa. More information about Chinese for U.S. citizens can be found at https://travel.state.gov/content/passports/en/country/china.html.

- Hershey Park, Hershey, Pennsylvania (www.hersheypark.com) – Fly into Harrisburg, Pennsylvania (MDT), which is about 15 miles from Hersey. You can also fly into Philadelphia (PHL) or Baltimore (BWI) then rent a car.

- Rye Playland, Rye NY (www.ryeplayland.org) – Fly into Westchester County Airport (HPN) and rent a car for the less-than-30-minutes' drive. Alternatively, you may fly into the other five New York-area airports (JFK, Islip (ISP), LaGuardia (LGA), Newark-Liberty (EWR)). A car will be necessary regardless of the airports. You could also take Amtrak to the Stamford, Connecticut, station and then rent a car and drive down to Rye.

- SeaWorld

- o Orlando, Florida (www.seaworldparks.com/en/seaworld-orlando/) – Fly into Orlando, FL (MCO), then rent a car.
- o San Antonio (https://seaworldparks.com/en/seaworld-sanantonio) – Fly into San Antonio (SAT), then rent a car.
- o San Diego (www.seaworldparks.com/en/seaworld-sandiego) – Fly into San Diego (SAN), then rent a car. The park is also accessible via public transit, and your hotel may have a free shuttle bus service.
- Six Flags (www.sixflags.com). The Six Flags brand has several parks around the U.S., Canada, Mexico, the Middle East, and People's Republic of China. I've highlighted a few of them below:
  - o Six Flags over Texas, Arlington, Texas (https://www.sixflags.com/overtexas?gclid=CO6GmLvflNECFdi1wAodjqILew) – This is the original park in the Six Flags family. The park took its theme from the flags of the six

countries that have held sovereignty over Texas
in its history: Spain, France, Mexico, the
Republic of Texas, U.S., and the U.S.
Confederacy. Fly into Dallas-Fort Worth
(DFW), then rent a car.

o Dubai in Dubai, United Arab Emirates,
(https://content.sixflags.com/dubai/). Slated to
open in 2019, this will be part of the Dubai
Parks and Resorts development
(www.dubaiparksandresorts.com/EN) – Fly
into Dubai (DXB), then rent a car.

o Fiesta Texas in San Antonio
(www.sixflags.com/fiestatexas) – Fly into San
Antonio (SAT), then rent a car to get to the
park.

o Great Adventure in Jackson, New Jersey
(www.sixflags.com/greatadventure) – Fly into
Philadelphia (PHL) or Newark-Liberty, New
Jersey (EWR), then rent a car. NJ Transit also
offers express bus service from New York City
and Newark, New Jersey, to the park.

o Great America in Gurnee, Illinois,
(www.sixflags.com/greatamerica) – Fly into

Chicago-O'Hare (ORD) or Chicago-Midway (MDW) and rent a car. You can also use Milwaukee (MKE) as a backup airport.

- o New England in Agawam, Massachusetts (www.sixflags.com/newengland) – Fly into Hartford, Connecticut (BDL), then rent a car. Alternate airports are Boston (BOS) or Albany, New York (ALB).
- o Over Georgia in Atlanta (www.sixflags.com/overgeorgia) – Fly into Atlanta (ATL) and rent a car.
- Valleyfair in Shakopee, Minnesota, (www.valleyfair.com) – Fly into Minneapolis/St. Paul-(MSP) and then rent a car.
- Warner Bros. Movie World in Gold Coast, Queensland, Australia (www.movieworld.com.au/) – Fly into Gold Coast, Queensland, Australia (OOL), and rent a car.
- Wet 'n Wild Orlando in Orlando, Florida (www.wetnwildorlando.com) – Fly into Orlando, Florida (MCO), and rent a car to the International Drive location.

- Wildwater Kingdom in Aurora, Ohio
  (www.wildwaterfun.com/) – Fly into Cleveland
  (CLE), and then rent a car.

33. Visit family and friends unexpectedly

O.K., you have something that a very small
percentage of the population has: You can travel at
the drop of a hat. So, go see your friends and family
at the last minute. You will be shocked at how much
they do appreciate the short visit. If you cannot meet
them at home, meet them in the airport while you
connect through their city. Or just do a quick turn.

I once met a friend of mine in the Atlanta (ATL)
airport; I was coming from Johannesburg (JNB) and
had a stop in Atlanta before going on to Houston.
When I was in Jo'burg airport, I contacted him and
advised that I was passing through. He agreed to
come and have a quick bite. I even surprised him
more and brought him a bottle of Amarula; a liqueur
from South Africa. He was quite pleased.

Of all the things I can do as an airline employee,
this one is my all-time favorite. There's nothing like
surprising your family and friends. The fun thing is
that all my family and friends are now surprised when
I visit for more than a day or so ☺. Not sure if that's
not a good thing…

34. Visit a U.S. national monument or memorial that is in a city other than your own

The U.S. is full of monuments; the Park Service alone has 149 of them listed on its Web site at www.nps.gov/archeology/sites/antiquities/monuments list.htm for starters. The Travel Channel has also listed some here at www.travelchannel.com/destinations/us/photos/us-memorials-and-monuments, so you have plenty to choose from. I'll help you get started with just a few of them:

- **Devil's Tower, Wyoming** – www.nps.gov/deto/index.htm. Fly into Gillette, Wyoming (GCC), on Delta (DL) or United (UA), then rent a car. You may also fly into Rapid City, Iowa (RAP), on American (AA), Delta (DL), or United (UA), and rent a car.

- **The Grand Canyon National Park, Arizona** – www.nps.gov/grca/index.htm. The closest airport is Flagstaff, Arizona (FLG). It's only served by American (AA). Then you can rent a car. You may

of course fly in Phoenix-Sky Harbor (PHX) or Las
Vegas (LAS) and then drive.

- **Martin Luther King, Jr. Memorial,
  Washington, D.C.** –
  www.nps.gov/mlkm/index.htm. While you are
  there, there are countless other monuments for you
  to visit. Fly into Washington-Reagan National
  (DCA), Washington-Dulles (IAD), or Baltimore-
  Washington (BWI) airports, then take the Metro or
  a bus to the Metro to check out these monuments.
  The nearest Metro station is the Smithsonian
  Station. Then it's a 20 minutes' or so walk to the
  monument.

- **The 9/11 Memorial New York City** –
  www.911memorial.org/. Fly into one of the New
  York-area airports (ISP, JFK, LGA, EWR) or even
  White Plains (HPN) and then take the NYC
  Subway system down to the World Trade Center
  area.

- **USS Arizona Memorial Honolulu** –
  www.nps.gov/valr/index.htm. Fly into Honolulu
  (HNL). Loads are usually quite bad, so check

back-up flights on this one. You can get there from many of the U.S. hubs for the larger U.S. airlines, and you can also get there from Canada as well, in case you get bumped. A fun way to get there is to head to Tokyo-Narita (NRT) and then to Honolulu on Delta (DL), Japan Airlines (JL), or United (UA).

So there you have it: many monuments to see. Now get out there and see them.

35. Watch a sports game played by your favorite team in another city, just because you can

This one is even easier than the previous one. Just pull up the Web site for your team, check when they have their away games, check your schedule and your pass agreements, and you are on your way. Oh, make sure tickets are available.

This one is all about you, so only you can make this happen.

36. Visit a remote place

I enjoy travel. OK, that's an understatement. Remote places fascinate me. These are places where it either takes either a long time or various modes of transportation to get there.

I hate planning, but some of these will take some planning. Here are a few of these places to consider. I'm sure you can find some more:

- Try Caye Caulker (CUK) and Ambergris Caye (SPR) in Belize – You can fly into Belize (BZE) with service from American Airlines (AA), Avianca (AV), Copa Airlines (CM), Delta Air Lines (DL), Southwest Airlines (WN), and United Airlines (UA). Once in Belize, you can take local airlines Mayan Air (MY) and Tropic Air (9N) from the international airport or the domestic airport Belize City (TZA) to the neighboring islands. Alternatively, you might head into Belize City and take a boat to the islands. It's interesting to watch the mainland disappear behind you and all around you is just water, and you now have to

trust that the boat handler knows where he's
going.

- Punta Arenas, Chile (PUQ). A few years ago in the
middle of their winter, July, I headed down to the
end of the world. Well, kind of. Punta Arenas is
the southernmost city in the world. Ushuaia,
Argentina (USH), is technically the southernmost
city in the world, except though it's not connected
to the rest of the continent as it is actually on an
island. To get to Punta Arenas, you fly on
LATAM (LA) from Santiago, Chile (SCL). This
area is quite remote. So remote that you can see
the stars at night very clearly without any
interference. If you go in July though, it's
wintertime, so dress appropriately.

- Loreto, Mexico (LTO). I went to a resort here
called Villa Del Palmar
(www.passrider.com/villadelpalmar). It is quite
remote as it's on the other side of the town of
Loreto. You take a 30-minute drive from the
airport served by Alaska Airlines (AS), Cabo San
Lucas-based Aero Calafia, and WestJet (WS).

Loreto is in the Baja, California, Sur peninsula,
and this was my first time here. The terrain is like
the Arizona desert area, and the only thing around
the resort is the resort. They take you out on a
boat to see whales and dolphins. While you are
out there, it's just you and the others in the boat
and the boat and the ocean with the coast line way
in the distance. At nights, it's crystal clear, and
you can see every constellation in the sky. Yes,
it's quite remote.

- The Marshall Islands. These islands and atolls are
located in the Pacific Ocean. Getting there is not
easy at all, but doable. Majuro (MAJ) is the
capital and is served by United Airlines (UA) as
part of its Island Hopper from Guam (GUM) to
Honolulu (HNL). If you are a diver, you will love
this area. Kwajalein (KWA) is another of the
Marshall Islands, and, although served by United,
you cannot get off on this island unless you are
U.S. military or invited by the people of that
island.

37. Take the United Airlines Island Hopper

When I mentioned that you visit Alaska in an
earlier chapter, that multi-stopper only has four stops.
This one, that used to be flown by Continental
Micronesia until the merger of Continental and
United, has five between Guam and Honolulu:

- Guam (GUM)
- Chuuk, Federated States of Micronesia (TKK)
- Pohnpei, Federated States of Micronesia (PNI)
- Kosrae, Federated States of Micronesia (KSA)
- Kwajalein, Marshall Islands (KWA)
- Majuro, Marshall Islands (MAJ)
- Honolulu (HNL)

The flight used to stop in Johnson Atoll, but it no
longer does. When it did stop there, as it's a U.S.
military base, you were not allowed to get off and had
to close the windows while the airplane was at the
base.

You won't get a seat unless they can clear you all
the way from GUM to HNL or vice versa as they
don't want to leave you on one of the islands along
the way. It's a great flight though as it's a little over

15 hours. You get to know the crew like a family when you get to either end. It's a great flight to take at some point.

Oh, you won't be able to get off the airplane in Kwajalein as it's a military base. But you'll be able to in the other islands, though briefly depending on how the operation is going.

It is now run by a Boeing 737-800, but it used to be a Boeing 727-200. I happen to have flown on both aircraft types and flew in both directions, and its pretty amazing. The best leg was flying off of Chuuk with full payload. We basically flew right off the edge of the island. What a rush!

38. Visit a city within one degree of the equator

This one is tough, but it is doable. It's something
different to do, but it takes a bit of research. Here are
your city choices if you decide to do this one:

- Pekanbaru, Indonesia (PKU) from
  - Jakarta, Indonesia (CGK), on Batik Air (ID),
    Garuda Indonesia (GA), and Lion Air (JT)
  - Kuala Lumpur, Malaysia (KUL), on Air Asia
    (AK)
  - Singapore (SIN) on Jetstar Asia (3K) and
    SilkAir (MI)
  - Plus service from other local Indonesian cities
- Libreville, Gabon (LBV) from
  - Addis Ababa, Ethiopia (ET), on Ethiopian (ET)
  - Casablanca, Morocco (CMN), on Royal Air
    Maroc (AT)
  - Istanbul (IST), on Turkish Airlines (TK)
  - Johannesburg (JNB) on South African Airlines
    (SA)
  - Lagos, Nigeria (LOS), on ASKY Airlines (KP)
  - Paris-Charles de Gaulle (CDG) on Air France
    (AF)

- o Plus other African carriers
- São Tome, São Tome and Principe (TMS) from
  - o Accra, Ghana (ACC), on TAP Portugal (TP)
  - o Libreville, Gabon (LBV), on CEIBA Intercontinental (C2 and Equaflight Gabon (L8)
  - o Malabo, Equatorial Guinea (SSG), on CEIBA Intercontinental (C2)
  - o Praia, Cape Verde (RAI), on TAAG Angola Airlines (DT)
- Entebbe and Kampala, Uganda (EBB), from
  - o Abu Dhabi, United Arab Emirates (AUH), on Etihad Airways (EY)
  - o Addis Ababa, Ethiopia (ADD), on Ethiopian Airlines (ET)
  - o Amsterdam (AMS) on KLM Royal Dutch Airlines (KL)
  - o Cairo (CAI) on EgyptAir (MS)
  - o Doha, Qatar (DOH), on Qatar Airways (QR)
  - o Dubai, United Arab Emirates (DXB), on Emirates (EK) and FlyDubai (FZ)
  - o Istanbul (IST) on Turkish Airlines (TK)

- o Johannesburg (JNB) on South African Airways (SA)
- o Kilimanjaro, United Republic of Tanzania (JRO), on FN (FN)
- o Nairobi, Kenya (NBO) on East African Safari Air Express (B5), Five Forty Aviation (5H), Kenya Airways (KQ), and Rwandair Express (WB)
- Mbandaka, Democratic Republic of the Congo (MDK), from
  - o Gemena, Democratic Republic of the Congo (GMA), on CAA Congo (BU)
  - o Kinshasa N'Djili, Democratic Republic of the Congo (FIH), on CAA Congo (BU)
- Macapa, Brazil (MCP) from
  - o Belem, Brazil (BEL), on Azul Brazilian Airlines (AD), Gol Transportes Aéreos (G3) and LATAM Brazil (LA)
  - o Brasilia, Brazil (BSB), on Gol Transportes Aéreos (G3) and LATAM Brazil (LA)
- Pontianak, Indonesia (PNK) from

- Jakarta, Djakarta ID (CGK), on Batik Air (ID), Citilink Indonesia (QG), Garuda Indonesia (GA), Lion Air (JT) and Sriwijaya Air (SJ)
- Quito, Ecuador (UIO) from
  - Atlanta (ATL) on Delta Air Lines (DL)
  - Bogota, Colombia (BOG) on Avianca (AV), Copa Airlines (CM), and TAME Linea Aerea del Ecuador (EQ)
  - Buenos Aires, Argentina (EZE), on TAME Linea Aerea del Ecuador (EQ)
  - Dallas/Fort Worth (DFW) on American Airlines (AA)
  - Fort Lauderdale, Florida (FLL), on JetBlue Airways (B6)
  - Guayaquil, Ecuador (GYE), on Aerolineas Argentinas (AR), Amazonas Airline (Z8), Avianca (AV), Iberia Airlines (IB), KLM Royal Dutch Airlines (KL), Lan Ecuador (XL), and TAME Linea Aerea del Ecuador (EQ)
  - Havana (HAV) on TAME Linea Aerea del Ecuador (EQ)
  - Houston-Intercontinental (IAH) on United Airlines (UA)

- o Lima, Peru (LIM), on Avianca (AV) and
  LATAM (LA)
- Kismaayo, Somalia (KMU), from
  - o Mogadishu, Somalia (MGQ), on Jubba
    Airways (3J)
- Yaren District, Nauru (INU), from
  - o Brisbane, Australia (BNE), on Nauru Airlines
    (ON)
  - o Lungga Guadalcanal Island, Solomon Islands
    (HIR), on Nauru Airlines (ON)
  - o Nadi, Fiji (NAN), on Nauru Airlines (ON)
  - o Kiribati (TRW) on Nauru Airlines (ON)
- Padang, Indonesia (PDG) from
  - o Jakarta, Djakarta, Indonesia (CGK), on Batik
    Air (ID), Citilink Indonesia (QG), Garuda
    Indonesia (GA, Lion Air (JT), and Sriwijaya
    Air (SJ)
  - o Jeddah, Saudi Arabia (JED), on Garuda
    Indonesia (GA)
  - o Kuala Lumpur, Malaysia (KUL), on Air Asia
    (AK)

If you can't make it to these cities, then you can
try these more popular ones that are within 10 degrees
of the equator either way:

- Abuja, Nigeria (ABV) from
  - Accra, Ghana (ACC), on Arik Air (W3)
  - Addis Ababa, Ethiopia (ADD), on Ethiopian
    Airlines (ET)
  - Cairo (CAI) on Egyptair (MS)
  - Dubai, United Arab Emirates (DXB), on
    Emirates (EK)
  - Frankfurt, Germany (FRA), on Lufthansa
    German Airlines (LH)
  - Istanbul (IST) on Turkish Airlines (TK)
  - Johannesburg (JNB) on South African Airways
    (SA)
  - London-Heathrow (LHR) on British Airways
    (BA)
  - Nairobi, Kenya (NBO), on Kenya Airways
    (KQ)
  - Paris-Charles de Gaulle (CDG) on Air France
    (AF)
- Accra, Ghana (ACC) from

- o Abidjan, Côte d'Ivoire (ABJ), on Arik Air (W3), Emirates (EK) and South African Airways (SA)
- o Addis Ababa, Ethiopia (ADD), on Ethiopian Airlines (ET)
- o Amsterdam (AMS) on KLM Royal Dutch Airlines (KL)
- o Barcelona, Spain (BCN), on Vueling (VY)
- o Beirut, Lebanon (BEY), on Middle Eastern Airlines (ME)
- o Brussels (BRU) on Brussels Airlines (SN)
- o Cairo (CAI) on Egyptair (MS)
- o Casablanca, Morocco (CMN), on Royal Air Morac (AT)
- o Dubai, United Arab Emirates (DXB), on Emirates (EK)
- o Istanbul (IST) on Turkish Airlines (TK)
- o Johannesburg (JNB) on South African Airways (SA)
- o Lagos, Nigeria (LOS), on Africa World Airlines (AW), Arik Air (W3), Rwandair Express (WB), and TAP Portugal (TP)
- o Lisbon, Portugal (LIS), on TAP Portugal (TP)

- o London-Heathrow-(LHR) on British Airways
  (BA)
- o Nairobi, Kenya (NBO), on Kenya Airways
  (KQ)
- o New York-JFK (JFK) on Delta Air Lines (DL)
- o Washington Dulles (IAD) on South African
  Airways (SA)
- Addis Ababa, Ethiopia (ADD), from
  - o Abuja, Nigeria (ABV), on Ethiopian Airlines
    (ET)
  - o Accra, Ghana (ACC), on Ethiopian Airlines
    (ET)
  - o Bangkok-Suvarnabhumi (BKK) on Ethiopian
    Airlines (ET)
  - o Beijing-Capital (PEK) on Ethiopian Airlines
    (ET)
  - o Beirut, Lebanon (BEY), on Ethiopian Airlines
    (ET)
  - o Cairo (CAI) on Egyptair (MS) and Ethiopian
    Airlines (ET)
  - o Cape Town, South Africa (CPT), on Ethiopian
    Airlines (ET)
  - o Delhi (DEL) on Ethiopian Airlines (ET)

- o Doha, Qatar (DOH), on Ethiopian Airlines (ET) and Qatar Airways (QR)
- o Dubai, United Arab Emirates (DXB), on Emirates (EK), Ethiopian Airlines (ET), and FlyDubai (FZ)
- o Dublin (DUB) on Ethiopian Airlines (ET)
- o Entebbe, Kampala, Uganda (EBB), on Ethiopian Airlines (ET)
- o Frankfurt, Germany (FRA), on Ethiopian Airlines (ET)
- o Guangzhou, People's Republic of China (CAN), on Ethiopian Airlines (ET)
- o Hong Kong (HKG) on Ethiopian Airlines (ET)
- o Istanbul (IST) on Turkish Airlines (TK)
- o Jeddah, Saudi Arabia (JED), on Ethiopian Airlines (ET), Lufthansa German Airlines (LH), and Saudi Arabian Airlines (SV)
- o Kuwait City (KWI) on Ethiopian Airlines (ET)
- o Lagos, Nigeria (LOS), on Ethiopian Airlines (ET)
- o London-Heathrow (LHR) on Ethiopian Airlines (ET)
- o Madrid (MAD) on Ethiopian Airlines (ET)

- o Mumbai (Bombay), India (BOM), on Ethiopian
  Airlines (ET)
- o Muscat, Oman (MCT), on Ethiopian Airlines
  (ET)
- o Nairobi, Kenya (NBO), on Ethiopian Airlines
  (ET), Kenya Airways (KQ), and Saudi Arabian
  Airlines (SV)
- o Paris-Charles de Gaulle (CDG) on Ethiopian
  Airlines (ET)
- o Riyadh, Saudi Arabia (RUH), on Ethiopian
  Airlines (ET) and Saudi Arabian Airlines (SV)
- o Rome-Fiumicino (FCO) on Ethiopian Airlines
  (ET)
- o São Paulo (GRU) on Ethiopian Airlines (ET)
- o Shanghai-Pu Dong, People's Republic of China
  (PVG), on Ethiopian Airlines (ET) Check
- o Tel Aviv, Israel (TLV), on Ethiopian Airlines
  (ET)
- o Vienna (VIE) on Ethiopian Airlines (ET)

Here is another list of cities you can try as well:

- Bogota, Colombia (BOG)

- Colombo, Sri Lanka (CMB)

- Dar es Salaam, Tanzania (DAR)

- Davao City, Philippines (DVO)

- Denpasar, Bali Indonesia (DPS)

- Freetown, Sierra Leone (FNA)

- Georgetown, Guyana (GEO)

- Guayaquil, Ecuador (GYE)

- Iquitos, Peru (IQT)

- Jakarta, Indonesia (CGK)

- Kandy, Sri Lanka (CMB)

- Kuala Lumpur, Malaysia

- Lagos, Nigeria

- Majuro, Marshall Islands

- Male, Maldives (MLE)

- Nairobi, Kenya (NBO)

- Panama City (PTY)

- Phuket, Thailand (HKT)

- San Jose, Costa Rica (SJO)

- Singapore (SIN)

39. Snorkel or scuba the Great Barrier Reef in Australia

One of the places I like in the world is the Great Barrier Reef. It's so vast, and the story behind it is even more amazing.

I remember my Guide saying that the shoreline used to be where we were exploring the reef. When you look back at where the shoreline was, one could only marvel at how all that occurred.

The closest airport is Cairns, Australia (CNS), in the north. When Continental Micronesia flew from Guam (GUM) a few times a week, it was much easier. Now the route is no longer served by the merged airline, United (UA), so you have to be more creative.

The easiest way is to get to Brisbane, Australia (BNE), and then take a flight up to Cairns. Of course, you can also get there from Melbourne (MEL) and Sydney (SYD); both have nonstop services from the U.S. and many other international cities. Here are some other ways to get to Cairns:

- Auckland, New Zealand (AKL), on Air New Zealand (NZ) or Philippine Airlines (PR)

- Brisbane, Australia (BNE), on Cathay Pacific
  Airways (CX, Jetstar Airways (JQ, Qantas (QF),
  Tiger Air Australia (TT), and Virgin Australia
  (VA)
- Hong Kong (HKG) on Cathay Pacific Airways
  (CX) and Hong Kong Airlines (HX)
- Manila (MNL), on Philippine Airlines (PR)
- Melbourne, Australia (MEL), on Jetstar Airways
  (JQ), Qantas (QF), Tiger Air Australia (TT), and
  Virgin Australia (VA)
- Osaka, Japan (KIX), on Jetstar Airways (JQ)
- Singapore (SIN) on SilkAir (MI)
- Sydney (SYD) on Jetstar Airways (JQ), Qantas
  (QF), Tiger Air Australia (TT), and Virgin
  Australia (VA)
- Tokyo-Narita (NRT) on Jetstar Airways (JQ)

While in that region, ensure that you visit the town
of Cairns. It's a sleepy town with lots of beauty. Take
a side trip and head up to Kuranda. It's best to rent a
car or take the Skyrail Rainforest Cableway up through
the rain forest, and take the Kuranda scenic railway
down. You can find more details at www.kuranda.org.

40. Visit Petra, Jordan

One of my ex-colleagues and I took a trip to Petra once. It was his idea. I just wanted to go to Jordan as a friend of mine had a meeting there, and it was a great time to catch up with each other and log a new country, airline, and airport.

We flew into Amman, Jordan (AMM), on Royal Jordanian (RJ) from Chicago-O'Hare (ORD) on a ZED fare. It was a great flight and my first time on Royal Jordanian.

My ex-colleague suggested that we head down to Petra as he'd always wanted to go, so of course I said yes. We hired a car and a driver and headed south to Petra. We had no idea what we would see, and we were in for a real treat.

We made several stops on the way down, including a spot from where we could see Bethlehem, Israel, in the distance. It was an odd feeling seeing a place you've only read about in the Bible.

Eventually, we made it to Petra, and it was worth the journey. It's like nothing we had ever seen before, so I implore you to go see it for yourself. You can

always fly into any of the European airport hubs and
then connect into Amman.

While there, try to see Wadi Rum if you can
(http://na.visitjordan.com/Wheretogo/Wadirum.aspx).
You do need another day in order to make this happen.
We did not make it as we took quite a while in Petra
and had only one day left in our stay.

There are places to stay in Petra overnight, so you
don't have to head all the way back to Amman. Check
www.passrider.com/hotelscombined.

If you need additional information, head over to
Visit Jordan's Web site at
http://na.visitjordan.com/Wheretogo/Petra.aspx.

41. Visit all the U.S. Presidential Libraries

Exiting U.S. Presidents have their own libraries. They are places where you can study the contributions the Presidents made to the U.S. I have an ex-colleague who loves to visit these libraries. I've actually only been to one of them: the John F. Kennedy Presidential Library and Museum in Boston. It's actually a beautiful place. I went with my parents ages ago, and they had a really good time as well.

Here's where to start www.archives.gov/presidential-libraries as it lists them all. Here's a look at where they are and how to visit them:

- Herbert Hoover Presidential Library Museum – www.hoover.archives.gov. West Branch, Iowa. The nearest airports are:
  - Cedar Rapids, Iowa (CID), with service from Atlanta (ATL) on Delta Air Lines (DL); Chicago-O'Hare (ORD) on American Airlines (AA), and United Airlines (UA); Dallas/Fort Worth (DFW) on American Airlines (AA); Denver (DEN) on Frontier Airlines (F9) and

United Airlines (UA); Detroit-(DTW) on Delta Air Lines (DL); Minneapolis/St. Paul (MSP) on Delta Air Lines (DL)

o Moline, Illinois (MLI) with service from Atlanta-(ATL) on Delta Air Lines (DL); Chicago-O'Hare (ORD) on American Airlines (AA) and United Airlines (UA); Dallas/Fort Worth (DFW) on American Airlines (AA); Denver (DEN) on United Airlines (UA); Detroit (DTW) on Delta Air Lines (DL); Minneapolis/St. Paul (MSP) on Delta Air Lines (DL).

- FDR Presidential Library & Museum – https://fdrlibrary.org. Hyde Park, New York. The nearest airports are:
  o Newburg, New York (SWF), with service from Detroit (DTW) on Delta Air Lines (DL); Fort Lauderdale, Florida (FLL), on JetBlue Airways (B6); Orlando, Florida (MCO), on JetBlue Airways (B6); Philadelphia (PHL) on American Airlines (AA).
  o As this location is upstate New York, you can fly into any of the four New York City-area

airports (JFK, LaGuardia (LGA), Newark-Liberty (EWR) and West Chester County (HPN)), take Metro North Railroad to Poughkeepsie, and then take a cab. There's also a free shuttle from the station called the Roosevelt Ride that will take you to the library and its surroundings.

- Harry S. Truman Library & Museum – www.trumanlibrary.org. Independence, Missouri. The nearest airport is:
  - Kansas City, Missouri (MCI), with service from Air Canada (AC) and all the U.S. airlines, except Allegiant and Virgin, from all their major hubs.
- Dwight D. Eisenhower Presidential Library, Museum and Boyhood Home – www.eisenhower.archives.gov. Abilene, Kansas. The nearest airports are:
  - Salinas, Kansas (SLN), with service from Denver (DEN) on Great Lakes Airlines (ZK)

- o Manhattan, Kansas (MHK), with service from
  Chicago-O'Hare (ORD) and Dallas/Fort Worth
  (DFW) on American Airlines (AA)
- o Wichita, Kansas (ICT), with service from
  Atlanta (ATL) on Delta Air Lines (DL);
  Chicago-O'Hare (ORD) on American Airlines
  (AA) and United Airlines (UA); Dallas/Fort
  Worth (DFW) on American Airlines (AA);
  Denver (DEN) and Houston-Intercontinental
  (IAH) on United Airlines (UA); Las Vegas
  (LAS) on Southwest Airlines (WN);
  Minneapolis/St. Paul (MSP) on Delta Air Lines
  (DL); Phoenix (PHX) and St. Louis (STL) on
  Southwest Airlines (WN).

- John F. Kennedy Presidential Library and Museum
  – www.jfklibrary.org. Boston. The nearest airport
  is:
  - o Boston (BOS) with service from all the U.S.
    airlines and several international airlines.
- Lyndon Baines Johnson Library and Museum –
  www.lbjlibrary.org. Austin, Texas. The nearest
  airport is:

- o Austin, Texas (AUS), with service from all the
  U.S. airlines from their hubs and a few
  international airlines with service from
  Frankfurt, Germany (FRA), on Condor (DE),
  Guadalajara, Mexico (GDL), on Volaris (Y4),
  London-Heathrow (LHR) on British Airways
  (BA), and Toronto (YYZ) on Air Canada (AC).
- Nixon Presidential Library & Museum –
  www.nixonlibrary.gov. Yorba Linda, California.
  The nearest airports are:
  - o Orange County, California (SNA), with service
    from almost all the U.S. airlines from their
    hubs
  - o Ontario, California (ONT), with service from
    Chicago-Midway (MDW) on Southwest
    Airlines (WN); Dallas/Fort Worth (DFW) on
    American Airlines (AA); Denver (DEN) on
    Southwest Airlines (WN)-and United Airlines
    (UA); Guadalajara, Mexico (GDL), on
    Aeromexico (AM) and Volaris (Y4); Houston-
    Intercontinental (IAH) on United Airlines
    (UA); Las Vegas (LAS) and Oakland,
    California (OAK), on Southwest Airlines

(WN); Phoenix (PHX) on American Airlines
(AA) and Southwest Airlines (WN); Portland,
Oregon (PDX), on Alaska Airlines (AS) and
Southwest Airlines (WN); Sacramento,
California (SMF), on Southwest Airlines
(WN); Salt Lake City (SLC) on Delta Air Lines
(DL); San Francisco (SFO) on United Airlines
(UA); San Jose, California (SJC) on Southwest
Airlines (WN); Seattle (SEA) on Alaska
Airlines (AS).

o   Long Beach, California (LGB), home to
JetBlue (B6) with service from Anchorage,
Alaska (ANC), Austin, Texas (AUS), Boston
(BOS), Las Vegas (LAS), New York-JFK
(JFK), and Oakland, California (OAK). Also
service on Southwest Airlines (WN) from
Phoenix (PHX), service on American Airlines
(AA) from Portland, Oregon (PDX), Reno,
Nevada (RNO), Sacramento, California (SMF),
Salt Lake City (SLC), and service on Delta Air
Lines (DL) from San Francisco (SFO) and
Seattle (SEA).

o Los Angeles (LAX) West Coast hub/focus city
  of American (AA), Delta Air Lines (DL) and
  United (UA) and served by all the U.S. carriers
  and many major international airlines.

o Burbank, California (BUR), with service from
  Dallas-Love Field (DAL) on Southwest
  Airlines (WN); Denver (DEN) on Southwest
  Airlines (WN) and United Airlines (UA); Las
  Vegas (LAS) on Southwest Airlines (WN);
  New York-JFK (JFK) on JetBlue Airways
  (B6); Oakland, California (OAK), on
  Southwest Airlines (WN); Phoenix (PHX) on
  American Airlines (AA) and Southwest
  Airlines (WN); Portland, Oregon (PDX), on
  Alaska Airlines (AS) and Southwest Airlines
  (WN); Sacramento, California (SMF), on
  Southwest Airlines (WN); Salt Lake City
  (SLC) on Delta Air Lines (DL); San Francisco
  (SFO) on Southwest Airlines (WN) and United
  Airlines (UA); San Jose, California (SJC), on
  Alaska Airlines (AS) and Southwest Airlines
  (WN); Seattle (SEA) on Alaska Airlines (AS).

o Palm Springs, California (PSP), with service
from Calgary, Alberta, Canada (YYC) on
WestJet (WS); Chicago-O'Hare (ORD) on
American Airlines (AA) and United Airlines
(UA); Dallas/Fort Worth (DFW) on American
Airlines (AA); Denver (DEN) on United
Airlines (UA); Edmonton, Alberta, Canada
(YEG) on WestJet (WS); Houston-
Intercontinental (IAH) and Los Angeles (LAX)
on United Airlines (UA); Minneapolis/St. Paul
(MSP) on Delta Air Lines (DL) and Sun
Country Airlines (SY); New York-JFK (JFK)
on JetBlue Airways (B6) and Virgin America
(VX); Phoenix (PHX) on American Airlines
(AA); Portland, Oregon (PDX), on Alaska
Airlines (AS); Salt Lake City (SLC) on Delta
Air Lines (DL); San Francisco (SFO) on
Alaska Airlines (AS), United Airlines (UA),
and Virgin America (VX); Seattle (SEA) on
Alaska Airlines (AS) and Delta Air Lines (DL);
Toronto (YYZ) on Air Canada (AC) and
WestJet (WS); Vancouver, British Columbia,
Canada (YVR), on Air Canada (AC) and

WestJet (WS); Winnipeg, Manitoba, Canada (YWG), on WestJet (WS).

- San Diego (SAN), with service from almost all the U.S. airlines from their hubs and a few international airlines with service from Calgary, Alberta, Canada (YYC), on WestJet (WS); Frankfurt, Germany (FRA), on Condor (DE); Guadalajara, Mexico (GDL), on Volaris (Y4); London-Heathrow (LHR) on British Airways (BA); Mexico City (MX) on Volaris (Y4); Tokyo-Narita (NRT) on Japan Airlines (JL); Toronto-(YYZ) on Air Canada (AC); Vancouver, British Columbia, Canada, on Air Canada (AC) and WestJet (WS); and Zurich (ZRH) on Eidelweiss Air (WK).

- Gerald R. Ford Presidential Library & Museum – www.fordlibrarymuseum.gov. The library is located in Ann Arbor, Michigan, and the Museum in Grand Rapids, Michigan. The nearest airport is:
  - Ann Arbor, Michigan – Detroit Metro Wayne (DTW), home to Delta Air Lines (DL) and served by all the U.S. airlines and Air Canada (AC).

o Grand Rapids, Michigan (GRR), with service from Atlanta (ATL) on Delta Air Lines (DL); Baltimore (BWI) on Southwest Airlines (WN); Charlotte, North Carolina (CLT), on American Airlines (AA); Chicago-Midway (MDW) on Southwest Airlines (WN); Chicago-O'Hare (ORD) on American Airlines (AA) and United Airlines (UA); Dallas/Fort Worth (DFW) on American Airlines (AA); Denver (DEN) on Southwest Airlines (WN) and United Airlines (UA); Detroit (DTW) on Delta Air Lines (DL); Fort Myers, Florida (RSW), on Southwest Airlines (WN); Houston-Intercontinental (IAH) on United Airlines (UA); Minneapolis/St. Paul (MSP) on Delta Air Lines (DL); New York-LaGuardia (LGA) on Delta Air Lines (DL); Newark-Liberty, New Jersey (EWR), on United Airlines (UA); Orlando, Florida (MCO), on Delta Air Lines (DL) and Southwest Airlines (WN); Philadelphia (PHL) on American Airlines (AA); Washington Dulles (IAD) on United Airlines (UA). The

airport in Grand Rapids is actually named after
President Ford.

- Jimmy Carter Presidential Library and Museum –
www.jimmycarterlibrary.gov. Atlanta. The nearest
airport is:
  - Atlanta (ATL) with service from almost all the
    U.S. airlines and several international airlines
    from around the world.
- Ronald Reagan Presidential Library & Museum –
https://reaganlibrary.gov/s-reasearch. Simi Valley,
California. The nearest airport is:
  - Burbank, California (BUR) with service from
    Dallas-Love Field (DAL) on Southwest
    Airlines (WN); Denver (DEN) on Southwest
    Airlines (WN) and United Airlines (UA); Las
    Vegas (LAS) on Southwest Airlines (WN);
    New York-JFK (JFK) on JetBlue Airways
    (B6); Oakland, California (OAK), on
    Southwest Airlines (WN); Phoenix (PHX) on
    American Airlines (AA) and Southwest
    Airlines (WN); Portland, Oregon (PDX), on
    Alaska Airlines (AS) and Southwest Airlines

(WN); Sacramento, California (SMF), on Southwest Airlines (WN); Salt Lake City (SLC) on Delta Air Lines (DL); San Francisco (SFO) on Southwest Airlines (WN)-and United Airlines (UA); San Jose, California (SJC), on Alaska Airlines (AS) and Southwest Airlines (WN); Seattle (SEA) on Alaska Airlines (AS).

o Los Angeles (LAX) West Coast hub and focus city of American (AA), Delta Air Lines (DL), and United (UA) and served by all the U.S. carriers and many major international airlines.

o Long Beach, California (LGB), home to JetBlue (B6) with service from Anchorage, Alaska (ANC), Austin, Texas (AUS), Boston (BOS), Las Vegas (LAS), New York-JFK (JFK), and Oakland, California (OAK). Additional service on Southwest Airlines (WN) from Phoenix (PHX), on Southwest Airlines; from Portland, Oregon (PDX), Reno, Nevada (RNO), Sacramento, California (SMF), and Salt Lake City (SLC) on American Airlines (AA); and from San Francisco (SFO and Seattle (SEA) on Delta Air Lines (DL).

- o Santa Barbara, California (SBA), with service
  from Dallas/Fort Worth (DFW) on American
  Airlines (AA); Denver (DEN) and Los Angeles
  on United Airlines (UA); Phoenix (PHX) on
  American Airlines (AA); Portland, Oregon
  (PDX), on Alaska Airlines (AS); San Francisco
  (SFO) on United Airlines (UA); Seattle (SEA)
  on Alaska Airlines (AS).

- o Ontario, California (ONT), with service from
  Chicago-Midway (MDW) on Southwest
  Airlines (WN); Dallas/Fort Worth (DFW) on
  American Airlines (AA); Denver (DEN) on
  Southwest Airlines (WN and United Airlines
  (UA); Guadalajara, Mexico (GDL), on
  Aeromexico (AM) and Volaris (Y4); Houston-
  Intercontinental (IAH) on United Airlines
  (UA); Las Vegas (LAS) and Oakland,
  California (OAK), on Southwest Airlines
  (WN); Phoenix (PHX) on American Airlines
  (AA) and Southwest Airlines (WN); Portland,
  Oregon (PDX), on Alaska Airlines (AS) and
  Southwest Airlines (WN); Sacramento,
  California (SMF) on Southwest Airlines (WN);

Salt Lake City (SLC) on Delta Air Lines (DL);
San Francisco (SFO) on United Airlines (UA);
San Jose, California (SJC), on Southwest
Airlines (WN); Seattle (SEA) on Alaska
Airlines (AS).

o Orange County, California (SNA), with service
from almost all the U.S. airlines from their
hubs

o Bakersfield, California (BFL), with service
from Denver (DEN) on United Airlines (UA),
Phoenix (PHX) on American Airlines (AA),
San Francisco (SFO) on United Airlines (UA).

o Palm Springs, California (PSP), with service
from Calgary, Alberta, Canada (YYC), on
WestJet (WS); Chicago-O'Hare (ORD) on
American Airlines (AA) and United Airlines
(UA); Dallas/Fort Worth (DFW) on American
Airlines (AA); Denver (DEN) on United
Airlines (UA); Edmonton, Alberta, Canada
(YEG), on WestJet (WS); Houston-
Intercontinental (IAH) and Los Angeles (LAX)
on United Airlines (UA); Minneapolis/St. Paul
(MSP) on Delta Air Lines (DL) and Sun

Country Airlines (SY); New York-JFK (JFK)
on JetBlue Airways (B6) and Virgin America
(VX); Phoenix (PHX) on American Airlines
(AA); Portland, Oregon (PDX), on Alaska
Airlines (AS); Salt Lake City (SLC) on Delta
Air Lines (DL); San Francisco (SFO) on
Alaska Airlines (AS), United Airlines (UA),
and Virgin America (VX); Seattle (SEA) on
Alaska Airlines (AS) and Delta Air Lines (DL);
Toronto (YYZ) on Air Canada (AC) and
WestJet (WS); Vancouver, British Columbia,
Canada (YVR), on Air Canada (AC) and
WestJet (WS); Winnipeg, Manitoba, Canada
(YWG), on WestJet (WS).

o San Diego (SAN), with service from almost all
the U.S. airlines from their hubs and a few
international airlines with service from
Calgary, Alberta, Canada (YYC), on WestJet
(WS); Frankfurt, Germany (FRA) on Condor
(DE); Guadalajara, Mexico (GDL); on Volaris
(Y4); London-Heathrow (LHR) on British
Airways (BA); Mexico City (MEX) on Volaris
(Y4); Tokyo-Narita (NRT) on Japan Airlines

(JL); Toronto (YYZ) on Air Canada (AC); Vancouver, British Columbia, Canada (YVR), on Air Canada (AC) and WestJet (WS); and Zurich (ZRH) on Eidelweiss Air (WK).

- George Bush Presidential Library and Museum – http://bush41.org. College Station, Texas. The nearest airport is:
  - College Station, Texas (CLL), with service from Dallas/Fort Worth (DFW) on American Airlines (AA) and Houston-Intercontinental (IAH) on United Airlines (UA)
- William J. Clinton Presidential Center and Park – www.clintonlibrary.gov. Little Rock, Arkansas. The nearest airport is:
  - Little Rock, Arkansas (LIT), with service from Atlanta (ATL) on Delta Air Lines (DL); Charlotte, North Carolina (CLT), on American Airlines (AA); Chicago-O'Hare (ORD) on American Airlines (AA) and United Airlines (UA); Dallas-Love Field (DAL) on Southwest Airlines (WN); Dallas/Fort Worth (DFW) on American Airlines (AA); Denver (DEN) on

United Airlines (UA); Detroit, (DTW) on Delta
Air Lines (DL); Houston-Intercontinental
(IAH) on United Airlines (UA); Las Vegas
(LAS), Phoenix (PHX), and St. Louis (STL) on
Southwest Airlines (WN).

- George W. Bush Presidential Library and Museum
  – https://georgewbushlibrary.smu.edu. Dallas. The
  nearest airport is:
  - Dallas/Ft. Worth (DFW), home to American
    Airlines (AA) and served by almost all the U.S.
    airlines from all their hubs.
  - Dallas/Love Field (DAL), home of Southwest
    Airlines (WN), has service from Atlanta (ATL)
    on Delta Air Lines (DL); and from Los
    Angeles (LAX), Las Vegas (LAS), New York-
    LaGuardia (LGA); San Francisco (SFO), and
    Washington (DCA) on Virgin America (VX).

42. Visit at least one of the world's tallest structures

One thing's for certain, our world loves to build tall buildings. And, as soon as one new tall building is revealed, you know another is being built somewhere. At the time of this writing The Freedom Tower in New York and the Willis Tower in Chicago were duking it out to see which was taller; Freedom Tower won. The views from these towers are always spectacular and well worth the trip.

Here are a few of the tallest buildings around the globe and how to find them:

- Burj Khalifa in Dubai, United Arab Emirates – www.burjkhalifa.ae/en/index.aspx
    o Fly into Dubai, United Arab Emirates (DXB), or Abu Dhabi, United Arab Emirates (AUH). From Abu Dhabi, you can take a 90-minute shuttle to Dubai.
    o Take the Metro to the Burj Khalifa stop.
    o Walk or take the local bus to the Palace Hotel, then make your way to the Burj Khalifa.

- o For a special treat, head up to the Atmosphere
  Lounge at the 123 floor; just one floor below
  the viewing area.
- The CN Tower in Toronto (YTO)
  - o Fly into Toronto-Billy Bishop (YTZ) or
    Toronto-Pearson (YYZ).
  - o You'll get great views of the stadium below,
    the city, the harbor, and the Billy Bishop
    Airport (YTZ).
- Empire State Building, New York (NYC)
  - o Fly into New York-Islip (ISP), New York-JFK
    (JFK), New York-LaGuardia (LGA), New
    York-Liberty (EWR), White Plains, New York
    (HPN)
- Freedom Tower in New York –
  www.oneworldobservatory.com
  - o Fly into New York-Islip (ISP), New York-JFK
    (JFK), New York-LaGuardia (LGA), New
    York-Liberty (EWR), White Plains, New York
    (HPN)
- The Menara KL Tower in Kuala Lumpur, Malaysia
  – www.menarakl.com.my

- o Fly into Kuala Lumpur, Malaysia (KUL).

- o This tower is often overlooked, but it should
  not be as it offers great views of the city below
  as well as the Petronas Towers itself.

- The Macau Tower in Macau –
  www.macautower.com.mo

  - o Fly into Macau (MFM) or take the ferries from
    Hong Kong. Visa is on arrival for U.S. citizens
    when entering Macau. No visa required for
    Hong Kong. Check with your local consulate
    for other citizenships.

- Petronas Twin Towers in Kuala Lumpur, Malaysia
  – www.petronastwintowers.com.my

  - o Fly into Kuala Lumpur, Malaysia (KUL).

- Shanghai Tower in Shanghai (SHA) [tallest in
  China]. There's also the Jin Mao Tower and the
  Shanghai World Financial Center, all in the same
  area.

  - o Fly into Shanghai-Pudong (PVG) or Shanghai-
    Hongqiao (SHA)

- The SkyTower in Auckland, New Zealand –
  www.skycityauckland.co.nz/attractions/sky-tower/

- o Fly into Auckland, New Zealand (AKL).

- Taipei 101 in Taipei, Taiwan – www.taipei-101.com.tw/en/index.aspx
  - o Fly into Taipei, Taiwan (TPE), the home of China Airlines (CI) and EVA Air (BR).

- Tokyo Skytree Tower in Tokyo, Japan – www.tokyo-skytree.jp/en/
  - o Fly into Tokyo-Haneda (HND) or Tokyo-Narita (NRT).

- Willis Tower in Chicago (CHI) – www.willistower.com
  - o Fly into Chicago-O'Hare (ORD) or Chicago-Midway (MDW).

43. Visit volcanoes

Our world has no shortage of volcanoes. For some reason as humans, we love to see them although we know they are quite dangerous and temperamental.

I've seen many from afar as I have no desire to climb them. For me their beauty is to view them from afar.

Here are a few of them you can enjoy either from afar or from climbing them, if it's allowed. Be careful as some of them could erupt at any time:

- Calbuco Volcano near Puerto Montt, Chile (PMC) – www.volcanodiscovery.com/calbuco.html. Fly in on LATAM (LA).
- Cumbre Vieja Volcano in Santa Cruz de Tenerife La Palma, Spain, in the Canary Islands (SPC) – www.volcanolive.com/lapalma.html.
- Kīlauea Volcano in the island of Hawai'i near the Hilo, Hawaii (ITO) airport – www.nps.gov/havo/index.htm.
- Mount St. Helens near Portland, Oregon (PDX) – www.mountsthelens.com. You can also fly into Seattle (SEA).

- Mount Vesuvius near Naples, Italy (NAP) –
  www.livescience.com/27871-mount-vesuvius-
  pompeii.html. When you visit Pompeii, you can
  get a great view of the mountain. My partner
  Walks of Italy provides a Vesuvius Tour. They
  also provide a tour of Pompeii as well.

- Head over to Passrider.com/tours for more details

- Volcan Pacaya in Guatemala. Fly into Guatemala
  City (GUA), then take local transport to Antigua –
  www.volcanpacaya.info.

- Volcan Arenal in Alajuela, San Carlos, Costa Rica.
  Fly into Libera (LIR) or San Jose (SJO) –
  www.arenal.net.

- Hike a dormant mountain in the valley of the
  Volcanoes in Ecuador. There are several volcanoes
  in Ecuador. Here are two to consider: Cotopaxi and
  Chimborazo. Fly into Quito (UIO) or Guayaquil
  (GYE) –
  www.volcanodiscovery.com/ecuador.html.

44. Fly on the world's longest flights

Years ago, I flew on Singapore Airlines' (SQ) Airbus A340-500 on the then-longest flight in the world: 18 hours from Newark-Liberty, New Jersey (EWR), to Singapore (SIN). That flight no longer exists today, but there are equally long flights around. Well, almost equally long. If none of these are your airlines, get a ZED fare and jump on one of them. The Singapore Airlines ZED was the most expensive one I've ever done at just over $500, but the experience was clearly worth it. Here are the current (as of this writing in January 2018) top 11 longest flights by distance. Get on one of them soon.

Rank	Details
1.	Qatar (QR) | 16:20 | DOH to AKL | 77L | 9,043 miles/14,554 kilometers
2.	Qantas (QF) | 18:20 | PER to LHR | 789 | 9,025 miles/14,522 kilometers (starts March 2018)
3.	United (UA) | 17:55 | LAX to SIN | 789 | 8,771 miles/14,116 kilometers

4. Emirates (EK) | 17:20 | AKL to DXB | 77L
| 8,834 miles/14,216 kilometers

5. United (UA) | 17:30 | IAH to SYD | 789 |
8,596 miles/13,834 kilometers

6. Qantas (QF) | 16:55 DFW to SYD | 380 |
8,590 miles/13,824 kilometers

7. Singapore Airlines (SQ) | 16:20 | SFO to
SIN | 350 | 8,447 miles/13,594 kilometers

8. United Airlines (UA) | 16:20 | SFO to SIN
| 789 | 8,447 miles/13,594 kilometers

9. Delta Air Lines (DL) | 15:16 | ATL to JNB
| 77L | 8,436 miles/13,598 kilometers

10. Etihad (EY) | 16:40 | LAX to AUH | 77L |
8,387 miles/13,498 kilometers

KEY

AKL – Auckland, New Zealand | AUH – Abu Dhabi,
United Arab Emirates | DFW – Dallas/Ft. Worth USA |
DOH – Doha, Qatar | DXB – Dubai, United Arab
Emirates | HKG – Hong Kong | IAH – Houston-

Intercontinental, TX USA | JED – Jeddah, Saudi
Arabia | JNB – Johannesburg, South Africa | LAX –
Los Angeles, CA USA | PER – Perth, Australia | PTY
– Panama City, Panama | SFO – San Francisco, CA
USA | SYD – Sydney, Australia.

380 – Airbus A380 | 77L – Boeing 777-200LR | 77W
– Boeing 777-300ER | 789 – Boeing 787-9

Airline Employee Before You Quit

45. Visit the Swedish Lapland

I've heard much about Lapland, but never experienced it until just recently. It is a vast area that sits about 64 degrees north latitude. To get to the area I visited, you first have to get to Stockholm, which has four airports: Arlanda (ARN), the largest served by the major European airlines as well as Delta and United; Bromma (BMA) served by Braathens Regional (TF), British Airways (BA), Brussels Airlines (SN), and Finnair (AY); Skavsta (NYO) served by Ryanair and WizzAir; and Västerås (VST) served by NextJet (2N), Ryanair (FR), and WowAir (WW).

Stockholm is a whole destination in and of itself and highly recommended. But let's press on and head north.

You can take a train; Swedish Rail or take a flight on NextJet (2N) to the Hemavan-Tarnaby Airport (HMV). NextJet is the only commercial airline that serves this tiny airport. The airline uses a British Aerospace ATP, which hold 68 passengers in a two-two configuration. Check with your pass bureau to see if you have any agreements with them; otherwise, you will have to buy a ticket at www.nextjet.se.

So what do you do when you get to Hemavan? It's a town of 150 inhabitants; however, during the winter ski season, it gets to about 2,500! Visitors come from all over as this is a premier ski lodge. You can find more information about the skiing at www.hemavantarnaby.se/en/skiing-in-hemavan-tarnaby/. There are ski resorts in Hemavan and also in Tarnaby, so take your pick.

In the summer, it's a hiker's paradise as it's the start of the longest trail in Sweden, the Kungsleden Trail, which runs for 425 kilometers. The air quality along these trails is amazingly fresh with pure mountain water coming from the streams along the way. And it's all drinkable. As I write this, I really want to go back very soon.

If you are into fishing, this is your place. As matter of fact, they do helicopter fishing where you are flown into a location to fish as it's not accessible by roads. You can fish in the summer and winter. The types of fish include Canada char, arctic char, trout, and whitefish.

One really cool thing that I did when I visited was to take a helicopter ride, organized by the Hemavan Tarnaby Tourism Board, to a town called Saxnas. The trip was about 41 minutes with amazing scenery. We even got a chance to see some reindeers that were on the slopes. They prefer the cold, so they were hanging out on some un-melted ice areas on the mountains. This same helicopter is actually used to herd them when the times comes around. The company we used is called Norr Helikopter. You can find information at www.norrhelikopter.se.

One cool thing to do in the Swedish Lapland if you are up for it is mountain snorkeling. Yes, it's exactly what it sounds like: You go snorkeling in the mountains. Our guide, Nils who runs the tour company, will suit you up in snorkeling gear and wetsuits. Then you hike the river and plunge in when the water is deep enough. There's even a spot where you can dive off a rock near a waterfall. That area is very deep. As you snorkel, you may see the local fish of the area (arctic char and trout) if you are lucky. I was lucky enough to see a few of them.

As if that was not enough, you can take a hike to
see the Arctic fox. These are an endangered species,
so you have to sign some special documents saying
that you won't trouble them, mess with their natural
habitat, or reveal their exact location. It's quite a trek
to get to where they are located. The area is also
infested with mosquitos and all kinds of bugs. It's
cold as well and takes quite the hike to get there; but
it's an easy sloping hike though. Not to worry though,
as Nils provides you with proper clothing and
coverage and as much mosquito repellant as you
require. Despite that, you have to keep brushing
mosquitos from around your head. It even gets more
interesting as you have to keep still so the foxes don't
hear you as, if they do, they won't come out.

On our trip, we did not see any, but we did see an
amazing sunset at 11:45p. It was a full-moon night so
there was also a spectacular moon rise on one side of
the mountain and the sunset on the other side.

There are not many hotels in Saxnas. I stayed at
the Saxnasgarden, which has a hostel on the same
property. You can find information at www.saxnas.se.
Just the scenery around this area is worth it. The lakes

are like mirrors and are perfectly still most of the times, making for great views and photos.

This is perhaps one of the coolest things that you can do as an airline employee before you quit since visiting Lapland is on many peoples' bucket lists.

46. Tour the headquarters of the major airplane manufacturers

I've had the great opportunity to tour the Airbus
plant and the Boeing plant. I even went on a roll-out
for the Boeing 757-300 as a guest of an employee
from Boeing and watched the roll-out for the Boeing
767-400 from across the street in Everett,
Washington. I also did a delivery flight for a Boeing
767-200, so I've had more than my fair share of
touring the manufacturers' plants.

It's so much fun to have these experiences, and,
since we have the means to check them out, we really
should. Here is some information to help you:

- Airbus – The Airbus company headquarters is in
  Toulouse, France (TLS), right at the airport. They
  also have facilities in Bremen, Germany (BRE),
  and Hamburg (HAM). Tours can be arranged for
  each of these facilities by checking their Web site
  at www.airbus.com/company/aircraft-
  manufacture/how-is-an-aircraft-built/. These are
  three great cities with lots to do when you visit, so
  give yourself a little extra time.

- Bremen is served by Air France (AF), bmi Regional (BM), Germania (ST), Germanwings (4U), KLM (KL), Lufthansa (LH), Ryanair (FR), SAS (SK), SunExpress (SQ), and Turkish Airlines (TK).

- Hamburg is served by Aegean (A3), Aer Lingus (EI), Aeroflot (SU), Air France (AF), Air Malta (KM), Air Serbia (JU), AirBaltic (BT), atlasglobal (KK), BlueAir (0B), British Airways (BA), Brussels Airlines (SN), Condor (DE), easyJet (U2), Emirates (EK), Eurowings (EW), Finnair (AY), Germanwings (4U), Germania (ST), Iran Air (IR), KLM (KL), Links Air (W2), LOT Polish (LO), Lufthansa (LH), Norwegian Air Shuttle (DY), Ryanair (FR), SAS (SK), SkyWork Airlines (SX), Swiss Airlines (LX), Tarom (RO), TAP Portugal (TP), TUIfly (X3), Turkish Airlines (TK), United (UA), VLM (VG), and Vueling (VY)

- Boeing in Seattle (SEA)
  - Fly into Seattle-Tacoma (SEA) or Seattle-Boeing Field (BFI) rent a car, and head up to

Everett, Washington, to visit the plant. There's also air service to Paine Field which is the same runway used by Boeing. So it's a short cab ride to the Touring facility.

Conversely, you can also fly into Vancouver, British Columbia, Canada (YVR), rent a car, and head down to Everett, Washington.

Here's a look at air service to the area airports:

o   Seattle-Boeing Field (BFI) is served by Kenmore Air (M5)

o   Seattle-Paine Field (PAE) will be served by Alaska Airlines (AS), Southwest Airlines (WN) and United Airlines (UA)

o   Seattle-Tacoma (SEA) is served by the following North American carriers: Aeromexico (AM), Air Canada (AC), Alaska Airlines (AS) [home town airline], American Airlines (AA), Delta Air Lines (DL), Frontier (F9), Hawaiian Airlines (HA), JetBlue (B6), Southwest Airlines (WN), Spirit Airlines (NK), Sun Country Airlines (SY), United Airlines (UA), Virgin American (VX) and Volaris (Y4). The

following international carriers also has
service: Aer Lingus (EI), Air France (AF),
All Nippon Airlines (NH), Asiana Airlines
(OZ), British Airways (BA), Condor (DE),
EVA Airways (BR), Emirates (EK),
Eurowings (EW), Hainan Airlines (HU),
Icelandair (FI), KLM Royal Dutch Airlines
(KL), Korean Airlines (KE), Lufthansa
German Airlines (LH), Norwegian Air
Shuttle (DY), Virgin Atlantic Airways
(VS), Virgin Australia (VA), Xiamen Air
(MF)

- o Vancouver, British Columbia, Canada
  (YVR), is served by: Aeromexico
  (AM), Air Canada (AC), Air China
  (CA), Air France (AF), Air New
  Zealand (NZ), Air North (4N), Air
  Transat (TS), Alaska Airlines (AS),
  All Nippon Airlines (NH), American
  Airlines (AA), Beijing Capital Airlines
  (JD), British Airways (BA), Cathay
  Pacific Airways (CX), Central
  Mountain Air (9M), China Airlines

(CI), China Eastern Airlines (MU), China Southern Airlines (CZ), Condor (DE), EVA Airways (BR), Eidelweiss Air (WK), Hong Kong Airlines (HX), Hainan Airlines (HU), Helijet International (JB), Icelandair (FI), InterJet (4O), Japan Airlines (JL), KLM Royal Dutch Airlines (KL), Korean Airlines (KE), Lufthansa German Airlines (LH), Pacific Coast Airlines (8P), Philippine Airlines (PR), Qantas (QF), Sichuan Airlines (3U), Sunwing Airlines (WG), United Airlines (UA), WestJet (WS) and Xiamen Air (MF).

47. Have a drink at the Ice Bar

There are a few ice bars around the world, and they are worth visiting. The idea is that you go into a bar made out of ice and have a drink like you would at any other bar. As it's pretty cold in there, you can only stay in for about 15 minutes to a half hour, and you have to dress warm.

Usually, they provide a hat, coat, boots, and gloves too. I experienced the one in Oslo, and it was a lot of fun. You can find more details about the ice bars at www.icehotel.com/about-icehotel/icebar/. Here are the details of a few of them:

- ICEBAR by ICEHOTEL
  - Jukkasjärvi, Sweden – ICEHOTEL, Marknadsvägen 63, Jukkasjärvi. The closest airport is Kiruna (KRN), which is served by Norwegian and SAS from Stockholm-Arlanda (ARN). Then you'd have to rent a car or take a taxi to get to the ICEHOTEL and then ICEBAR. There may be local shuttle service for the 14 minutes' drive, but just check with the hotel.

- o London (LCY, LGW, LHR, LTN, SEN, STN)
  – 31-33 Heddon St, London W1B 4BN. Oxford
  Circus is the closest Tube stop. Then walk
  down Regent Street to Heddon.
- o Oslo, Norway (OSL) – Kristian IV's gate 12
  0164 Oslo. Fly into Oslo, the home of
  Norwegian (DY) and SAS (SK), on most
  European airlines as well as United (UA).
  Then, take the train from the airport into the
  city, where you can take a taxi to the ICEBAR
  or just walk from the city center. You can also
  take the 1, 2, 3, 4, or 5 Tram to Stortinget
  station, and then it's a short walk. More details
  at www.icebaroslo.no/en/.
- o Stockholm (ARN) – Vasaplan 4, 111 20
  entrance via Nordic Sea Hotel lobby.
  - • You have no shortage of airlines flying into
    Stockholm-Arlanda (ARN) airport,
    including Delta and United. Once at
    Arlanda, you can take the Arlanda Express
    into the city, then it's a short walk to the
    ICEBAR at the Nordic C Hotel. There is

also Swedish Rail and an airport bus to get
to the city.

- There's also the Stockholm-Bromma
  airport (BMA) with flights from Belgium,
  Denmark, Finland, and within Sweden on
  British Airways (BA), Brussels Airlines
  (SN), Finnair (AY), and Scanwing (TF).
- Lastly, you can fly into Stockholm-Skavsta
  (NYO), which is 100 kilometers south of
  Stockholm. There is an airport bus that will
  take you into the city as well.

48. Hike to the tops of the pyramids of Tikal in Guatemala

Central America and Mexico have many locations
where you can experience the remains of the Mayan
culture. I've visited a few in Mexico; however, there
are also some in Central America, namely Guatemala.

Tikal, Guatemala, is home to a Mayan pyramid.
The area is actually the largest excavated site in the
Americas and also a UNESCO Heritage site. You can
find more details at www.mayan-ruins.org/tikal/.

To get here, you can fly into the Tikal/Flores
(FRS) airport from Belize City, Belize (BZE), on
Tropic Air (9N) or from Guatemala City (GUA) on
Avianca (AV) or Royal Belau Airways (5U). Then
get local transportation to the pyramids.

Get out there and enjoy these ruins and learn about
a different ancient culture.

49. Visit the 49th parallel between the U.S. and Canada

My first time seeing the 49th parallel amazed me as all I could think of was two countries living in harmony with no fences between them. I say "seeing", but there is not really a line to see as such. Think of it as an empty, green, flat field with trees on either side of the field. And as far as you could see in one direction, it's empty. It seems to go on forever, although you know it does not.

In the other direction and where I'm standing, there's a building which houses the officials. Here you present your documentation and are given the go-ahead to cross the border. It's so different than arriving at an airport in a foreign country.

There is an actual road, Roosevelt Way, that serves as the dividing line between the two countries. Canadians live on the north side and Americans on the south. You could ask your neighbor in another country for some salt if you needed it.

Further down this road is an actual monument that marks the location of the 49th parallel. It is on the

right as Roosevelt Way turns left and becomes Marine
Dr. So how do you get here?

Fly into Vancouver, British Columbia, Canada
(YVR), or into Seattle (SEA) and then drive to Point
Roberts, Washington. Point Roberts is actually in the
U.S., in Washington state; however, you can only
access it by ferry from the U.S. mainland or via road
from Canada.

If you arrive from Vancouver, head south and
follow the signs to Point Roberts. If you land in
Seattle, head north, cross the U.S./Canadian border,
turn left off the major road heading to Vancouver, and
head south to Point Roberts.

Once you cross the border into the U.S., turn right,
drive to the end of that road, Roosevelt Way; you will
see the monument for the 49th parallel.

Take some additional time to drive around the
town and see if you can spot the rest of the U.S. from
the shores. It's quite a quaint place to visit.

50. Fly on the world's shortest flight

A few years ago (2010), I had the distinct pleasure of flying the world's shortest flight. It plies from West Ray (WRY) to Papa Ray (PPW) in the Orkney Islands of Scotland. Loganair (LM), a Scottish Regional airline operates the flight, so check your pass agreement. You can check out my video of my experience at www.youtube.com/watch?v=tycz3A75hQ8.

The U.K. has considered building a bridge, but it looks like that's not yet the case. You can make the leap by ferry, too. Find more information at www.papawestray.co.uk/getting-to-papa-westray.html.

To experience this flight, head to Kirkwall (KOI) in the Orkney Islands and then take Loganair (LM) from Kirkwall for the flight over. Check Loganair schedule at https://www.loganair.co.uk/travel-information/orkney-inter-island-services/. Kirkwall is served by BMI Regional BM), flybe. (BE) and Loganair (LM).

You can get to Kirkwall from Aberdeen/Dyce, Scotland (ABZ); Bergen, Norway (BGO); Edinburgh,

Scotland (EDI); Glasgow, Scotland (GLA); Inverness,

Great Britain (INV); and the Shetland Islands,

Sumburg (LSI).

This is one of aviation's great experiences, so you

should check it out. If you do, let me know how it

went.

51. Attend a major airshow

We are aviation professionals, and one of the ways
we learn is by attending conferences and also
airshows. There are a number of large ones that are
worth attending, including:

a. **The Dubai Airshow** (DXB) –
http://www.dubaiairshow.aero/ – Usually held the
second week of November in Dubai, United Arab
Emirates. DXB Airport is the home of Emirates
Airlines (EK) and is served by Middle Eastern and
European carriers. From the U.S., you would either
have to take one of the Middle Eastern carriers
(Emirates (EK), Etihad (EY), or Qatar Airways
(QR) or fly into a European hub and get to Dubai
from there. If you fly into Abu Dhabi on Etihad,
you can take a shuttle into Dubai.

b. **The Dayton Airshow** (DAY) –
https://www.daytonairshow.com/ – Held in the
middle of June at the Dayton International Airport
in Dayton, Ohio, U.S.A. DAY airport is served by
most of the U.S. carriers.

c. **EAA Oshkosh** [Appleton (ATW), Green Bay (GRB)] – https://www.eaa.org/en/airventure – Held at the Oshkosh Airport (OSH) the end of July. I think this is the biggest airshow in the U.S. OSH is a general aviation airport. You can fly into ATW or GRB. Of course, if you have your own airplane, you can fly right into OSH. The airport provides a camping area so you can make a camping outing of the week-long event.

d. **The Farnborough Airshow** [Gatwick (LGW), Heathrow (LHR), London City (LCY), Luton (LTN), Stanstead (STN), Southend (SEN)] – http://www.farnborough.com/ – Held in Farnborough, England, at the Farnborough Airport (FAB), this event alternate years with the Paris Airshow, with Farnborough taking even years. Fly into one of the six London airports and take the train out to Farnborough. There is no sense in driving out there as traffic is horrendous. There are hotels in the area as well, but they tend to be quite full during the event.

e. **The Paris Airshow** [Paris-Beauvais (BVF), Paris-Charles de Gaulle (CDG), Paris-Orly (ORY)] –

http://www.siae.fr/en/ – Held at the end of June
every other year in odd years in Le Bourget,
France, just outside of Paris and near the Charles
de Gaulle Airport. This event flip-flops years with
the Farnborough Airshow. There are usually buses
from the Charles de Gaulle Airport to the show as
well as buses from the Le Bourget train station on
the RER B and from other key spots in Paris.

f. **The Reno Championship Air Race** [Reno
(RNO), Sacramento (SMF)] – http://airrace.org/ –
Held in Reno, Nevada, U.S.A., at Stead Air Field
in mid September. Fly into RNO, then rent a car or
take a local bus to the airfield. They may have
special transportation during the race from the
airport. You could also fly into Sacramento
International Airport in California (SMF) and rent
a car for the drive that takes two to three hours,
depending on the route you take.

g. **Oregon International Airshow** (PDX), Portland,
Oregon, U.S.A. – http://www.oregonairshow.com/
– Held at August/September at the Hillsboro
Airport in Portland, Oregon. You can take the Blue
Line out to the Airport stop and then walk about

five to 10 minutes to the entrance. Portland
International Airport is served by all the U.S.
airlines, so you have plenty of air support here.

h. **Singapore Airshow** (SIN), Singapore –
https://www.singaporeairshow.com/ – Held
biennially at the beginning or middle of February.
The next Singapore Airshow will be in 2018. As
Singapore is a major airport in Asia, you can get
there from almost every large airline and many
low-cost carriers. It's actually held at the
Singapore Airport. They close the airport for about
an hour to only airshow traffic. The show itself is
held at the Expo Center, which is near the airport.
http://singaporeexpo.com.sg/.

i. **Wings Over Houston Airshow**, Houston
[Houston-Hobby (HOU), Houston-Intercontinental
(IAH)] – http://www.wingsoverhouston.com/ –
This is held at the end of October at Ellington
Field, which used to be a commercial airport
served by Continental Airlines. For the airshow,
you can fly into HOU or IAH, rent a car, and drive
down to the airshow. HOU is closer.

52. Spend a day watching planes land and take off in St. Maarten (SXM)

If you love planes, you have to do this; if you do not like planes (I'm not sure who you are), you still have to do it.

The planes come in for a landing extremely close to the beach. You really have to see this to believe it. You can also relax and have a cold drink at the bar right on the beach. They have a surfboard which lists the times of the arriving flights, so you don't miss a beat. They now have a live camera (http://www.mahobeachcam.com/) you can watch, but you still need to go in person. What an atmosphere!

For added enjoyment, crazy tourists will try to hold onto the fence as the planes take off. Rest assured that you will see one or two of them being blown into the beach water nearby. Please don't copy these crazy people.

St. Maarten/St. Martin (SXM) is usually pretty tough to get to as a passrider, so check the loads before you go and look for back-up exits as well. It's a resort destination, so hotels are a bit pricey. From

the U.S., American (AA), Delta (DL), JetBlue (B6),
Seaborne (BB), Spirit (NK), and United (UA) serve
SXM. Then from Canada, it's Air Canada (AC), Air
Transat (TS) and Westjet (WS). Air France (AF)
comes in from Paris and KLM (KL) from
Amsterdam. A number of Caribbean airlines,
including Caribbean Airlines (BW), Liat (LI), Pan
Am World Airways Dominicana S.A (7N) and Winair
(WM), also serve the island, and Copa Airlines (CM)
comes in from Panama. Ensure you have back-up
passes, though, as it gets tricky. Once I had to buy a
ticket to St. Thomas (STT), then take American to
San Juan (SJU).

A cool side trip to make is to nip over to Saba
(SAB) on Winair (WM). You will love the landing
since it has the dubious honor of being the world's
shortest runway at 400 meters.

53. Spend four hours in Las Vegas just for the heck of it

Why not? The city is accessible from all major U.S. cities with nonstop flights. There are also a number of nonstop international flights as well: Aeromexico (AM) from Mexico City (MEX) and Monterrey, Mexico (MTY); Air Canada (AC) from Calgary, AB Canada (YYC), Montreal, QC Canada (YUL), Toronto, ON Canada (YYZ) and Vancouver BC Canada (YVR); British Airways (BA) from London-Gatwick (LGW) and London-Heathrow (LHR); Condor (DE) from Belfast International, Northern Ireland (BFS), Frankfurt, Germany (FRA), Glasgow, Scotland (GLA), London-Stanstead, England (STN) and Manchester, England (MAN); Copa Airlines (CM) from Panama City (PTY); Eidelweiss Air (WK) from Zurich, Switzerland (ZRH); Hainan Airlines (HU) from Beijing-Capital, Beijing PROC (PEK); InterJet (4O) from Guadalajara, Mexico (GDL), Mexico City, Mexico (MEX) and Monterrey, Mexico (MTY); Korean Airlines (KE) from Seoul, South Korea (ICN); Norwegian Air Shuttle (D8) from

Copenhagen, Denmark (CPH), London-Gatwick,
England (LGW), Oslo, Norway (OSL) and Stockholm-
Arlanda (ARN); LATAM (LA) from São Paulo, Brazil
(GRU); Virgin Atlantic Airways (VS) from London-
Gatwick, England (LGW) and Manchester, England
(MAN); VivaAerobus (VB) from Mexico City,
Mexico (MEX) and Monterrey, Mexico (MTY);
Volaris (Y4) from Guadalajara, Mexico (GDL) and
Mexico City (MEX); WestJet (WS) from Calgary, AB
Canada (YYC), Edmonton, AB Canada YEG),
Hamilton, ON Canada (YHM), Regina, SK Canada
(YQR), Saskatoon, SK Canada (YXE), Vancouver, BC
Canada (YVR) and Winnipeg, MB Canada (YWG).

Grab a flight after work, spend a few hours, and
then head back home via a red-eye flight. I suggest that
you decide how much money you want to spend before
you leave and stick to it. Vegas can become
addictive… Here are a few things you can do:

- Play poker or gamble. I'm not a gambler, but Las
  Vegas is the home of gambling.
- Ride the roller coaster at the New York-New York
  Hotel and Casino.

- Drive to the Nevada/California border to shop at the Outlet stores and ride the roller coaster out there. This may take more than four hours, though.

- Drink a beer on the Strip. The only other place you can really do this type of drinking in the street is New Orleans, Louisiana. Remember that the beer must be in a plastic bottle, otherwise you may be ticketed as no glass containers are allowed on the Las Vegas Strip even if you are not drinking alcohol.

- Take a quick trip out to see the Hoover Dam, but this will take longer than four hours unless it's the only thing you do and make it quick.

- Check out the High Roller. This is a Ferris wheel with pods. One of the pods is actually a bar, so you can drink for 30 minutes. The view is pretty amazing and if you're lucky and the winds are right you can see a landing to the airport.

- Watch the fountain show at the Bellagio Hotel and Casino.

I have written a few posts you can use to enhance your trip: http://www.cruisinaltitude.com/how-to-get-the-most-out-of-your-las-vegas-stay/ and

http://www.cruisinaltitude.com/travel-tip-tuesday-

alternate-things-to-do-in-las-vegas/.

54. See your favorite artist perform in a city other than your home city

This is quite a bit of fun and even more fun if you take your friends along with you on buddy passes. A colleague, a friend of his, and I once flew up to Columbus, Ohio (CMH), to see Janet Jackson perform. It was my first time to Columbus, so it was a new airport and a cool town. I actually visited the original Wendy's as well, so that was an unexpected side trip.

Another friend traveled to see Madonna, but I can't remember the city though.

Isn't this an easy one? Just think, you can easily hop on a flight, and, if the schedules work, you can hop back on a flight and head home the next day or even do a red-eye flight back, depending on where you are located and headed.

So, find out where your favorite artist is playing and make it happen.

55. Take your parents on a special unexpected trip

This is a pretty cool thing to do. I assure you they will be thrilled when you tell them this news. Of course, the more exotic the better. Just look on your airline's route map, pick a city, check the loads, and go. Or, better yet, check the availability and let that determine your choices.

If you can find a flight or flights with the front cabin open, that makes it even better.

Get going!

56. Decide on a Friday morning where you are going that Friday after work and actually do it

How easy is this one? You have the world at your fingertips, literally; so make the most of it.

It's actually easier to decide on a Friday or the same day you want to travel since, by then, you'll have a much better idea of the flight loads. Plus, most of the passriders would have already listed, so you can better see your chance of getting on a flight.

The worst that can happen is that you get to the airport, and that flight has filled up for operational reasons or others spotted the same flight and have listed as well. Then, you just pick a different city. Chances are they all won't be full. Don't forget to check the return loads, of course.

One thing to do is to always pack the following:

- Umbrella
- Swim wear
- Light jacket

This way, no matter where you decide to go, you are covered ☺.

57. Go to a major international sporting event

There is no shortage of sporting events to visit. You just need to remember that the flights and hotels will be limited. But you can fly to alternate cities or airports or attend the event in the early stages if it's something like World Cup Football or The Olympic Games.

Here is a list of events to consider:

- Formula 1 Racing – This event is held in several locations worldwide, so you just pick a location and head there. One of the best ones is Monaco. You'd fly into Nice, France (NCE), then take a helicopter, a bus, or the train to Monaco. You can find full details about all the events at www.formula1.com. Here's a list of the places where the races are held:
  - Austin, Texas (AUS)
  - Bahrain (BAH)
  - Baku, Azerbaijan (GYD)
  - Catalunya (BCN, GRO)
  - Hockenheim, Germany (FRA, STR)
  - Hungaroring, Hungary (BUD)
  - Kuala Lumpur, Malaysia (KUL)

- Melbourne, Australia (MEL)
- Mexico City (MEX)
- Monte Carlo, Monaco (NCE)
- Montreal (YUL)
- Monza, Italy (LIN, MXP)
- São Paulo (CGH, GRU, VCP)
- Shanghai (PVG, SHA)
- Silverstone, United Kingdom (BHX, DSA, EMA, LCY, LHR, LGW, LTN, SEN, STN)
- Singapore (SIN)
- Spa-Francorchamps, Belgium (BRU, CGN, DUS, LUX, MST)
- Spielberg, Austria (GRZ, VIE)
- Sochi, Russia (AER)
- Suzka, Japan (NGO, ITM, KIX)
- Yas Marina, Abu Dhabi, United Arab Emirates (AUH, DXB)

- Golf Championships – If you are a golf fan, the PGA Tour Web site at http://www.pgatour.com/tournaments/schedule.html lists all the tournaments throughout the year. Just pick one where the flights are open and get going.

- Summer Olympic Games – Held every four years
  with the next scheduled for Tokyo in 2020. Go to
  www.olympic.org for details.

- Winter Olympic Games – Held every four years,
  but not the same years as the summer games. The
  next is scheduled for Pyeongchang, South Korea,
  in 2018. Go to https://www.olympic.org/ for more
  details. After that, it's Beijing in 2022.

- Super Bowl – This is an American event, the
  annual championship game and culmination of the
  season. It's held every year at a different location,
  usually at the end of January or beginning of
  February. Details at www.nfl.com/superbowl.

- Tennis Open – There are four major events held
  every year. Extensive details on planning this trip
  are included elsewhere in this volume. You can
  find details about all the Opens at:
    o Australian Open Tennis – www.ausopen.com
    o French Open – www.rolandgarros.com
    o Wimbledon – www.wimbledon.com
    o U.S. Open – www.usopen.org

- Triple Crown (Horse Racing)

- Kentucky Derby – Louisville, Kentucky (SDF)
  – www.kentuckyderby.com
- Preakness Stakes – Baltimore (BWI, DCA,
  IAD) – www.preakness.com
- Belmont Stakes – Queens, New York (JFK,
  LGA, EWR, ISP, HPN) –
  www.belmontstakes.com

58. Get bumped from a flight

This one is quite easy; you may not have to even plan for it. Some pass riders have never been bumped from a flight, so they have no idea what to do. Treat this as a teaching tool if this is the case.

Once you get bumped, pick a new destination or come up with a creative routing to accomplish your task.

Just list for a flight you know you won't make as its already overbooked and there are a lot of people listed, or it has seats, but you are way down the list to even make the flight.

Then choose a new random destination. It's the spontaneity that works here. And, if you've never been bumped from a flight, it prepares you for it as, at some point in the future, it will happen.

59. Fly an airline other than your own, often

You'd be amazed at how many airline employees have never done this. This is a great way to absorb another country's culture in terms of food, people, movies, etc. It is always interesting to see how other airlines do things. We are all similar, but different all at the same time.

I really enjoyed flying Gulfair (GF) once from Doha, Qatar (DOH), to Bahrain (BAH) to Dubai, United Arab Emirates (DXB). It was very eye opening to see what the migrant workers used as luggage. It was basically plastic pails tied up in cloths. Works quite well, as a matter of fact.

If you can't get to your destination on your own carrier, flying Other Airline (OA) is a great way to do so using a ZED fare or an ID fare.

Introduce yourself to the cabin and flight crew and try to foster a relationship with your fellow airline employees. You never know, you may end up meeting again in the future. Exchanging emails is also a good idea so you can keep in touch later.

Often, they have really good ideas about places to stay, what to eat, what to do, and also where you may be able to get airline discounts. Plus, you can share the same ideas with them about your own country.

60. Take a trip with your co-workers

When I started working at American Trans Air
(ATA) in Indianapolis back in 1995, my co-workers
never traveled together. Instead, they would
occasionally go on trips organized by Ambassadair,
the ATA Travel Club. Although the airline is no
longer operating, the Travel Club
(https://www.ambassadair.com/) still exists and offers
exciting excursions.

I convinced my colleagues, who later became my
friends, to take a trip with me to Las Vegas for one
weekend night. Initially, they were skeptical, asking
the usual questions: Where will we stay, what will we
do, and so on.

I said, "Well, we don't have to stay anywhere
since we are taking the last flight out and the first
flight back."

We took that trip and have taken many trips
during my almost two years at ATA.

Over the years at different airlines, I continue to
travel with my colleagues. To this day I still travel
with my ex-colleagues when they are available.

You should try doing the same thing with your
colleagues. Traveling together creates a great bond
and allows you to learn so much about each other.
You-might even get closer.

Taking one of these trips also saves money as you
can split the expenses, so as not to leave anyone
holding the bag, I suggest that each person document
what they spend on group expenses and where.
During the flight back, dump them in a spreadsheet
and figure out how to divvy up the expenses. Create a
document on Google Docs and share it with the others
so they can all enter the information on what they've
spent. There are even some Apps now that can help
you determine this by sending money and also
allowing you to track your expenses during the trip
and reconcile later. Here are a few of them:

- Billr (Paid) Android | IOS (http://billr.me/)
- Cost Split (Free) (http://www.costsplitapp.com/)
  Android | IOS
- Kittysplit (Free Desktop)
  https://www.kittysplit.com/en/
- Splittr (Paid) Android | IOS

- Splitwise (Free) Android | IOS
(http://www.splitwise.com)
- Trip Splitter (Paid) Android | IOS
    http://www.dcsoftwarearts.com/tripsplitter
- Tripl.it | IOS
- Venmo (Free) Android | IOS

So now you've found another use for your computer
that you should take on your trips with you.

Your only obligation is to remember, "WHOTTSOTT"
applies; "What happen on the trip stays on the trip." I did
not come up with this acronym. An ex-colleague named
Matt did, and we all use it to this day.

61. Enjoy a beer festival or visit a brewery

There are more of these festivals and breweries around the world than you think. If you love beer, then you should try to visit at least a few of these.

Start by checking out the beer Festival Calendar. Yes, there is such a thing. You can find it at www.beerfestivals.org.

Here are some beer festivals to check out:

- Austin, Texas (AUS) BeerFeast
  www.saucerbeerfeast.com/festival?location=austin
- Denver (DEN)
  - o Denver Beer Fest www.denver.org/denver-beer-fest.
  - o Great American Beer Festival
    www.greatamericanbeerfestival.com/
- Edinburgh, Scotland (EDI, GLA) –
  http://www.edinburghcamra.org.uk/events/index.html. American (AA), Delta Air Lines (DL), and United (UA) all serve Edinburgh from the U.S. There are also connections from the European hubs.

- Fort Worth, Texas (DAL, DFW) BeerFeast
  www.saucerbeerfeast.com/festival?location=fort-
  worth

- London (LCY, LGW, LHR, LTN, SEN, STN) –
  The Great British Beer Festival http://gbbf.org.uk/.

- Munich (MUC) – Oktoberfest. I've been here once
  and totally loved it. Here's an article I wrote about
  the event – http://www.passrider.com/attraction-
  review-oktoberfest-whats-all-the-hype-about-6-
  things-you-should-know-from-a-local/.

- Portland, Oregon (PDX) – Oregon Brewers
  Festival www.oregonbrewfest.com

- Sugarland, Texas (HOU, IAH) – BeerFeast
  www.saucerbeerfeast.com/festival?location=sugar-
  land

Here is a list of some of the better brewery tours
around the globe:

Anheiser-Busch Budweiser Brewery Experience
The tours tell the story and the history of beer at
Anheiser-Busch. They do have an App you can
download to keep track of it all. In addition to tour
information, you can check in once you arrived for

your particular tour. The tours are held in the following cities:

- Fairfield, California (SMF, SFO, OAK, SJC) – 3101 Busch Drive, Fairfield, CA 94534. You can find additional information at www.budweisertours.com/locations/fairfield-california.html.

- Ft. Collins, Colorado (DEN, COS) – 2351 Busch Drive, Fort Collins, CO 80524. You can find additional information at www.budweisertours.com/locations/ft-collins-colorado.html.

- Houston (HOU, IAH) – 775 Gellhorn Drive, Houston, TX 77029. You can find additional information at www.budweisertours.com/locations/houston-texas.html.

- Jacksonville, Florida (JAX, DAB) – 111 Busch Drive, Jacksonville, FL 32218. You can find additional information at www.budweisertours.com/locations/jacksonville-florida.html.

- Merrimack, New Hampshire (MHT, BOS) – 221 Daniel Webster Highway, Merrimack, NH 03054. You can find additional information at http://www.budweisertours.com/locations/merrimack-new-hampshire.html

- St. Louis (STL) – 12th and Lynch Street, St. Louis, MO 63118. You can find additional information at www.budweisertours.com/locations/st-louis-missouri.html.

Guinness Storehouse

The Guinness Brewery tour in Dublin is also a pleasant experience. More details at https://www.guinness-storehouse.com/en. Located at St James's Gate, Dublin 8, Ireland, it is reachable by the #77A and #40 buses from the center of Dublin. Of course you can always take a cab or Uber if available.

If you go up to the top of the structure, and look out at the city, you are actually looking out from the froth that's at the top of any glass of Guinness. And, yes, you do get to sip a pint of Guinness before completing the tour. Plus, you see how to properly pour a pint. It's pretty fascinating.

You can fly into Dublin (DUB) or neighboring
Shannon, Ireland (SNN), to access this particular
brewery. Dublin is the home of Aer Lingus (EI) and
Ryanair (FR). From the U.S., American Airlines
(AA), Delta Air Lines (DL), and United Airlines
(UA) fly into Dublin/Shannon. If you fly into
Shannon, you can then fly to Dublin or take a bus
over. More details at
www.shannonairport.ie/gns/Passengers/Go/by-
bus.aspx.

The Heineken Experience

One of the more famous breweries in the world is
the Heineken Brewery located at Stadhouderskade 78,
1072 AE Amsterdam.

Dubbed the Heineken Experience
(www.heineken.com), you get to see how the beer is
made as well as receive samples before you leave. For
this one, you fly into Amsterdam Schipol (AMS),
then take the train into the city. Once at Centraal
Station, then take the 754 from Platform K. You may
also take the #16 or #24 Tram from platform A3.

Schipol is the home of KLM (KL) and a major hub in Europe so almost all the major airlines that fly into Europe serve Amsterdam.

From the U.S., American Airlines (AA), Delta Air Lines (DL), and United Airlines (UA) all fly into Schipol.

62. Go to at least one of the annual film festivals around the world

If you are into the arts or interested in visiting any of these destinations, then it's worthwhile to visit these film festivals. I've only been to Cannes, and I loved it. I must tell you, though, that the flights are packed during this time of the year to Nice, France (NCE), so be prepared to ride the train or find alternate airports to fly into. Typically Paris-to-Nice is almost impossible. It took us a few days when I went with two of my colleagues. We ended up flying into Lyon (LYS), staying overnight, and catching a flight the next morning. Nevertheless, we had a wonderful time. Here are some of the larger film festivals around the world:

- Austin Film Festival in Austin, Texas (AUS) – www.austinfilmfestival.com. Usually held in October. Fly into AUS and take a bus downtown or rent a car. Airport is served by most U.S. airlines as well as a few international airlines, including British Airways (BA).

- Festival de Cannes (Cannes Film Festival) in
  Cannes, France (NCE) – www.festival-cannes.fr.
  This is the crème de la crème of film festivals. The
  Hollywood heavy hitters usually attend. The
  festival is held at the end of May. It's challenging
  to get to Nice (NCE) at this time due to the loads.
  Also, it's vacation time for the French as well.
  Once you arrive in Nice, you can rent a car or take
  a bus down to Cannes. You can fly into Paris-
  Charles de Gaulle (CDG) and then take Air France
  (AF) down to NCE or you may also take the train.
  It's also possible to fly into other European hubs
  such as Frankfurt, Germany (FRA), and then head
  to Nice (NCE).

- Seattle International Film Festival in Seattle (SEA)
  – www.siff.net. Alaska Airlines (AS) is hubbed
  here. Fly into SEA and take the train to the
  downtown area for the cinemas.

- South by Southwest in Austin, Texas (AUS) –
  www.sxsw.com. This is usually hard to get to as
  the hotels and flights are usually full, and it's
  pretty pricey as well. However, there are tons of

parties, and it's a big social-media thing, if you are
into that. Fly into AUS and take a bus downtown
or rent a car. Airport is served by most U.S.
airlines as well as a few international airlines,
including British Airways (BA).

- Sundance Film Festival in Park City, Utah (SLC) –
www.sundance.org/festivals/sundance-film-
festival. Delta Air Lines (DL) is hubbed here. Fly
into SLC and take the train into the city. Most of
the U.S. airlines serves this airport as well.

- Telluride Film Festival in Telluride, Colorado
(TEX) – www.telluridefilmfestival.org Usually
held in early September, this is another cool place
to see the Hollywood stars. The Telluride airport is
your gateway, then take local transport into the
town. You can't get into the TEX airport
commercially so your nearest airport is
Montrose/Telluride (MTJ). Here are some details
about that airport as well as other neighboring
airports:

- o Montrose (MTJ) – Allegiant Air (G4)
  American Airlines (AA), Delta Air Lines (DL)
  ,and United Airlines (UA)
- o Cortez (CEZ) – Great Lakes Aviation (ZK)
- o Durango (DRO) – American Airlines (AA) and
  United Airlines (UA)
- o Grand Junction (GTJ) – Allegiant Air (G4)
  American Airlines (AA), Delta Air Lines (DL),
  and United Airlines (UA)
- o Gunnison Crested Butte (GUC) – United
  Airlines (UA)

- Tribeca Film Festival in New York –
  www.tribecafilm.com/festival/. I've not been to
  this one despite living in New York for quite some
  time. With New York having five airports (EWR,
  ISP, HPN, JFK, LGA), it makes it easier to get into
  the city and see the festival. There's train service
  from the airports or a cab into the city if you arrive
  at ISP.

63. Take your best friends and family on an "all air tickets paid" trip to an international destination

It's always great to treat families and friends to a trip. Usually the biggest thing holding them back is the airfare, and this is where you come in since you can give them a buddy pass, or, if they are a family member, they can travel as the same rate you do or at a very huge discount.

Watch those loads so you can have a hassle-free trip. If the flights fill up at the last minute, don't cancel the trip. Simply change the destination. This is what airline-employee travel is all about. But remember to manage the expectation of your guests. They may have their minds set on seeing Paris, but you end up in Amsterdam.

There is really nothing like taking your family and friends on an unexpected trip. Get them packed, get the necessary travel documents and health certificates if applicable, and, when they get to the airport, they will find out where they are going.

Try it. Let me know how it went.

64. Enter a country by air and exit by another means of transportation or vice versa

Europe makes it really easy to do this as there is air service into almost all the countries, and some of them even have water taxi service or ferries to other countries. One example that comes to mind is to fly into the U.K. and depart by ferry to Ireland:

When in London or any part of the U.K., purchase a ticket from the train station to Dublin. It will route you by train through Wales, which is really cool to see, and you pass the train station/town with the second longest name in the world, Llanfairpwllgwyngyllgogerychwyrndrobwllllantysilio gogogoch.

You get off at the end of the line in Hollyhead and take the Irish Ferries to Dublin, where you board a bus into the city. From there, you can spend the night, have a Guinness, and take your flight home from the Dublin Airport. You can also get a ticket to Shannon, Ireland, as well as Belfast, Northern Ireland, except that you would be back in the U.K. in Belfast.

Now you can buy your tickets separately (train and ferry), but it will cost you more, so don't do that.

In the United States and Canada, this can be accomplished by bus and/or train service and ferry services in if you are on the west coast of the U.S. and Canada.

Mexico has bus service to and from the United States, so that's totally doable.

There is also the possibility of cruise-ship services between countries. You can easily do this in Scandinavia. DFDS (https://www.dfdsseaways.com/) is the place to find these ferries.

So, you have plenty of options.

65. Take a red-eye flight and go to work that same day

I've done this countless times. It's a great way to maximize a weekend or your days off. It's also very risky since, if you get bumped off that red eye, you'll be late for work. So, ensure that you have checked the loads and have back-up flights in mind.

These are especially useful for those United States West Coast weekend trips as there's pretty much a red eye flight to the middle of the country or to the East Coast from each of the major West Coast cities.

This also works for Asia-to-Europe flights as well for flights from the U.S. East Coast to Europe.

If you can't sleep on planes, this will be difficult for you as you really need to get some sleep on the flight. If you have an airport or airline lounge card, you can take a shower or nip home really quick, grab a shower, and then head to work.

66. Go to a city and party 24 hours, then return home

You actually have several choices here; but I'll highlight only a few:

- *London from the U.S./Canada* – Take a day flight leaving between 8a and 9a local East Coast U.S. time that arrives in the U.K. about 8p or so. Go out on the town all night (the city does not sleep), then head for the airport the next morning. You can get a shower and shave (if applicable) by using the public showers at the airport or the showers in the airline/airport lounge (membership has its privileges), then sleep all the way back home. Careful not to get inebriated as you may be denied boarding.

- **In the reverse direction**, you can take a late flight out of Europe (say about 6p or later), then enjoy a night on the town in the U.S. or Canada, and take a day flight back home.

- *Heading to the West Coast* of the U.S. is a prime candidate as you can always take the red-eye flight back to your hometown.

- ***You can fly into London*** on a night flight arriving first thing the next morning, take the train to Paris, enjoy the city, and depart the next day back to your hometown. This is a bit more than 24 hours, though.

I'm sure you can think of other clever routings...

67. Take a trip and do not stay in a hotel

There are a few ways you can do this. Red-eye
flights make this quite easy. Thing 66 mentioned how
you can do some partying that does not involve a
hotel. But there are several day trips you can do or
overnight trips that work as well without the partying:

- If you fly to Las Vegas first thing in the morning
  and return on the last flight at night, you need no
  hotel.

- Take a red-eye flight from the U.S. West Coast to
  the U.S. East Coast, spend the day exploring the
  city, and take the last flight back home. Consider
  Boston, New York, Philadelphia, and Washington.

- Fly from Seattle, Portland, or Vancouver down to
  San Francisco, San Diego, or Los Angeles. There's
  lots to see and do in these cities before returning
  home. You can do the reverse as well. Each of
  these cities has either a bus and/or trains that goes
  directly to the airport from the city center.

- Don't be left out if you are in Europe as you can be
  in another country within a few hours either by
  train, bus, or an airplane. An example is London to

Paris, Frankfurt, Munich, Berlin, Prague, or
Stockholm. The possibilities are endless in Europe.

- If you are in Asia, you can hop over to Hong Kong
from Bangkok, Singapore, or Tokyo. You can even
do Tokyo to Singapore, then fly back on the first
flight of the morning.

- There's also Australia to New Zealand as well as
intra-Australia as you can do Sydney to Perth, or
Perth to Brisbane or Melbourne.

Let your imagination run wild. Use Passrider.com
to check the schedules before you go. Remember to
check the loads in both direction and be flexible.

68. Do something distinctly different because you can as an airline employee

I hope you can see that the theme of this book is for you to get out there and enjoy your benefits. You work hard and are in a position to have unique opportunities that others don't have. Why not make use of them? With that said, here are some more cool things you can do that are pretty unique as an airline employee:

a) Visit all the cities in the world whose names starts with the same letter as your first and or last name. While in these cities, try to find streets named after you. Or visit a city that has a street named after your first or last name. I've found Kerwin Street in Cairns, Australia. I have a friend called Lake, and there's actually a street called Lake that intersects with it. So I sent him a picture when I visited it. He was thrilled! I found McKenzie Drive in Point Roberts in Washington state. I took my Mom there, but she was not too thrilled; I bet my Dad would have been though ☺. Get out there and do something cool.

b) Visit the National Atomic Museum in New
Mexico.

- You can find additional information at
  http://www.nuclearmuseum.org

- You fly into Albuquerque, New Mexico
  (ABQ), which is served by the major U.S.
  airlines and Sun Country Airlines. Then rent a
  car and head out. The loads to ABQ gets very
  bad, so please check before you go.

c) At least once a year, visit somewhere you've never
visited before. This is an easy one. Just pick a
place, check the passport and visa requirements
(you can find this on the airline's Web site), check
which airline serves that place, check your
agreements with that carrier, check the loads,
purchase the passes, and go. Oh, and have fun.

d) Take a flight between two cities you've never
visited just for the heck of it. It's good to keep
track of it as well. This way, you can compare it
with friends and check the cities off as an
accomplishment.

e) Go to the airport and try to get on the first flight you see, without even checking the availability for the outbound or the return. This is risky as you may get stuck somewhere, so do it when you have plenty of time to get back to work. Try this on a Friday evening or a Saturday, for example, if you work Mondays through Fridays.

f) Fly in Economy class although Business/First class is available. For some of you out there, I know this is a tough one, but try it, if at least for the experience; Economy class is not all that bad. My friends think I'm crazy to even consider this as some of them won't even travel if Business or First class is not available. I've sat in the middle seat on many long flights. It's not too bad. At least it's a seat, right?

g) Be daring; do something different, such as zoom down the zip lines in the jungles of Montverde, Costa Rica, or in Roatan, Honduras. Just so you know, I'm not a fan of zip lines, but I recognize that we are all different ☺.

h) Run with the bulls in Pamplona, Spain (The Festival of San Fermin).

- This is very dangerous, but, if you like extreme events, this is not one to be missed. Follow the locals and stay out of the way of the horns of the bulls. You can find additional information at http://www.spanish-fiestas.com/spanish-festivals/pamplona-bull-running-san-fermin.htm. The festival starts on July 6th each year, and the first bull run happens July 7th. The last Run takes place July 14th.

- The nearest airport is Pamplona, Spain (PNA), which is three miles/four kilometers from the city and is served by Iberia (IB) and TAP Portugal (TP).

- I have not done this as yet, but that doesn't mean I won't. I may sit on the sidelines and watch it all transpire. I have a friend who has run with the bulls, and he had a blast! Just be careful out there.

i) Go snorkeling in Caye Caulker, Belize, in Shark-Ray Alley with the stingrays and nurse sharks.

- This is not for the faint of heart as you literally do swim with the sharks. Your boat is nearby,

but it is still creepy to see the manta rays and
sharks swimming right there. I was in the water
for all of 30 seconds; check. I was the
designated photographer for my group ☺.

- Fly into Belize City, Belize (BZE) using:
  o Air Canada (AC)
  o American Airlines (AA)
  o Avianca (AV)
  o Copa Airlines (CM)
  o Delta Air Lines (DL)
  o Royal Belau Airways (5U)
  o Southwest Airlines (WN)
  o Maya Island Air (2M)
  o Tropic Air (9N)
  o United Airlines (UA)
  o Westjet (WS)

Go into Belize City and take a local boat to
Caye Caulker or San Pedro. You may also take
Maya Island Air or Tropic Air between the
international airport and the local airport
downtown (TZA) as well as to the neighboring
islands. Watch for mosquitos as there are

plenty there. Get some mosquito repellant on
arrival.

69. Run a marathon or similar race in any city of your choice; especially Marathon, Greece

Throughout the year there are many marathons worldwide. If running is your passion, (it's not mine ☺), then how cool would it be to do one in a foreign city? Better yet, a foreign country! There's apparently a Web site for everything and, yup, there is one for marathons. You can find a list of marathons at http://www.marathonguide.com/races/races.cfm.

Some require committing well in advance, so check them out. Others have a lottery.

One of my ex-colleagues used to do races all over the world. Not necessarily marathons, but those three race things; biking, swimming, and then running. I'd follow along if I'd never been to that city before ☺. It was a lot of fun.

I also have many friends in Houston who periodically do marathons. You are all amazing!

70. Take a high-speed train

I enjoy trains. I've been taking trains since I was a little child. I'm always seeing out trains when I travel. There are many high-speed trains worldwide. just take your pick in your favorite city:

- Shanghai airport to downtown Shanghai – Once you arrive at the Shanghai International, follow the signs to the train. You arrive in downtown Shanghai in eight minutes with a top speed of 450 kilometers an hour.

- The Shinkansen in Japan (https://www.japan-guide.com/e/e2018.html) – These trains head out of the city to neighboring towns. Just pick one. I took one to Niigata and also to Nagoya.

- ICE in Germany – Try the Berlin-to-Hamburg route or the shorter Frankfurt-to-Cologne shuttle market. Either one you choose you will be whisking away at speeds of 300 kilometers an hour at some point in your journey. Lufthansa staff receive a discount by showing your ID.

- Eurostar in Europe – This train does the London-to-Paris run. I think they run faster on the French side, though.

- Frecciarossa in Italy (https://www.italiarail.com/frecciarossa) – You can take these trains from Rome to Milan or Rome to Naples, to name two routes. They are fantastic trains with top speeds of almost 300 kilometers an hour. You can enjoy First and Business class if you so desire. Even in Economy/Standard class, they are comfortable trains.

- TGV (http://www.sncf.com/en/trains/tgv) – These run intra-France and also to neighboring countries.

71. Go see the taping of a TV show

I've seen the taping of a few TV shows, and it's
pretty fascinating how it's all done. It's not what
you'd expect at all. I encourage you to visit a studio
somewhere around the world and be a part of the
audience. Here are a few worth checking out:

- the ellen degeneres show – The show is taped at
  the Warner Bros. Studios in Burbank, California.
  Airports close by are: BUR, LAX, LGB, ONT,
  SNA). You'll need to rent a car once you arrive at
  the airport. You can request tickets at
  http://www.ellentv.com/tickets/.

- The Graham Norton Show – The show is taped at
  the ITV Studios in London. Fly into LHR, LCY,
  LTN, SEN, or STN. You can request tickets at
  www.sroaudiences.com. Search for Graham
  Norton. There are other TV shows on the page as
  well.

- The Price is Right – The show is taped in
  Hollywood California, at CBS Television City. Fly
  into BUR, LAX, LGB, ONT, SNA. Get tickets at

http://on-camera-audiences.com/shows/The_Price_is_Right.

- The Tonight Show with Jimmy Fallon – The show is taped in New York. Fly into JFK, LGA, EWR, ISP, or HPN. You can request tickets at https://fallon.1iota.com/show/353/The-Tonight-Show-Starring-Jimmy-Fallon.

- Pick one of the many reality or game shows in existence today and sit through a taping.

72. Go golfing in some of the world's best golf courses

I'm not a golfer, but I've seen some amazing golf courses in my travels. I played golf once, and it was dismal. My score that is ☺. I must say I did enjoy it, although it was very tiring, and I think I had more beers than I played golf.

For the 2016 Olympic Games in Rio, I actually went to my first golf tournament. I must say I was quite impressed, and it was a lot of fun to partake in it. So, I do see the appeal. Still miffed by how they keep track of that small ball. It's also interesting to be standing by the holes and ball just drops in, plop... But I'm digressing.

One thing I've noticed is that a few airports have a golf course either on them or very close to them.

The world is full of many, many great golf courses. I could write a book just on those alone. However, I'll just name a few here to whet your appetite and get you started:

- Pebble Beach Golf Links, Pebble Beach, California, www.pebblebeach.com/golf/ – Alaska

Airlines (AS), American Airlines (AA), and United
Airlines (UA) serve the closest airport, which is
Monterey Regional (MRY). Other airports in the
area include San Jose (SJC), Fresno (FAT), San
Francisco (SFO), Oakland (OAK), San Luis
Obispo (SBP), and Bakersfield (BFL).

*   The Hawaiian Islands – There are several golf
    courses on the Hawaiian Islands. Check this Web
    site for locations: www.hawaiigolf.com/courses/.
    Honolulu (HNL) is the home of Hawaiian Airlines
    (HA), and each of the islands are served either
    nonstop from the U.S. mainland or with connecting
    service on Hawaiian Airlines (HA), Island Air
    (WP), or Mokulele Airlines (MW). International
    airlines such as Air Canada (AC), Air China (CA),
    Air New Zealand (NZ), ANA (NH), China Airlines
    (CI), China Eastern (MU), Fiji Airways (FJ), Japan
    Airlines (JP), Jetstar (JQ), Korean (KE), Philippine
    Airlines (PR), Qantas (QF) and WestJet (WS) also
    serve Honolulu (HNL). Just watch the loads as it's
    usually tricky to get to Hawaii as well as fly
    between the islands.

- St. Andrews Links, St. Andrews, Scotland
  www.standrews.com – The closest airport is
  Dundee, Scotland (DND), with service from flybe.
  (BE) from Amsterdam (AMS) and London-
  Stansted (STN). You can also fly into Edinburgh
  (EDI) or Glasgow (GLA) from the U.S. on
  American Airlines (AA), Delta Air Lines (DL), or
  United Airlines (UA). You can get public
  transportation to the train station in either city, take
  a train to Leuchars station, which is just outside of
  St, Andrews, and then take a bus or a cab to the
  courses. You can find additional information at
  www.standrews.com/getting-here.

- TPC at Sawgrass, Ponte Vedra Beach, Florida,
  www.tpc.com/sawgrass – The nearest airport is
  Jacksonville, Florida (JAX), which is served by all
  the larger U.S. airlines serving the East Coast of
  the U.S. Then rent a car and head south to the
  course.

- Torrey Pines, La Jolla, California,
  www.torreypinesgolfcourse.com – The nearest

airport is San Diego (SAN). Then rent a car and drive north on I-5 to get to the course.

- Mexico – There are a number of great golf courses in Mexico. Check out this Web site at www.top100golfcourses.co.uk/golf-courses/north-america/mexico. I did a visit to the Villa del Palmar Resort in Loreto, Mexico (LTO), that has this fantastic golf course being built. By the time you read this item, it will be complete. To get there, though, you fly from Los Angeles (LAX) to Loreto, Mexico (LTO), on Alaska Airlines (AS). Then, rent a car or take the paid hotel shuttle service to the resort. The holes are amazing. One you'll love is perched on the top of a cliff with an amazing view of the ocean. Head over to www.passrider.com/vpl for more details.

In addition, there are a few courses that are in close proximity to major airports. I have to give Golf Digest the credit here as they wrote an article about it at www.golfdigest.com/story/airportgolf_0504 and also leading courses at https://en.leadingcourses.com/. I've added some that I've seen on my travels though.

Here they are:

- Hartsfield-Jackson Atlanta International – Atlanta
  (ATL) – College Park Municipal Golf Course
  (3711 Fairway Drive, College Park). It's two miles
  from the airport. This is the home of Delta Air
  Lines (DL). The airport is served by many
  international carriers as well as U.S. domestic
  airlines.

- Bangkok-Suvarnabhumi International – Bangkok
  (BKK) – Thana City Golf & Sports Club. It's
  located 3.2 miles away. This is the hub of Thai
  Airways (TG). The airport is served by many
  international carriers.

- Chicago-O'Hare, Chicago (ORD) – White Pines
  Golf Course (500 W. Jefferson St., Bensenville).
  It's located two miles away. This is one of the hubs
  of American Airlines (AA) and the home of United
  Airlines (UA). The airport is served by many
  international carriers as well as U.S. domestic
  airlines.

- Dallas/Ft. Worth (DFW) – Bear Creek Golf Course (3500 Bear Creek Court). It's located six miles away. This is the home of American Airlines (AA). The airport is served by many international carriers as well as U.S. domestic airlines.

- Denver (DEN) – Green Valley Ranch Golf Course (4900 Himalaya Road). It's located 12 miles away. This is the home of Frontier Airlines (F9) and one of the hubs for United Airlines (UA). The airport is served by many international carriers as well as U.S. domestic airlines.

- Houston-Intercontinental, Houston (IAH) – Cypresswood Golf Course (21602 Cypresswood Drive, Spring). It's located six miles away. This is one of the hubs of United Airlines (UA). The airport is served by many international carriers as well as U.S. domestic airlines.

- Las Vegas McCarran, Las Vegas (LAS) – Bali Hai Golf Course (5160 Las Vegas Blvd. S) It's four miles away. The airport is served by many international carriers as well as U.S. domestic airlines.

- Minneapolis-St. Paul International, Minneapolis
  (MSP) – Hiawatha Golf Course (4553 Longfellow
  Ave. S., Minneapolis). It's located six miles away.
  This is the hone of Sun Country Airlines and one
  of the hubs of Delta Air Lines (DL). The airport is
  served by many international carriers as well as
  U.S. domestic airlines.

- Phoenix Sky Harbor, Phoenix (PHX) – ASU
  Karsten Golf Course (1125 E. Rio Salado Parkway,
  Tempe) www.asukarstens.com. It's five miles
  away which is about a 10-minute drive from the
  airport. Other courses in the area are: Papago
  (www.papagogolfcourse.net), The Raven at South
  Mountain and the Legacy Golf Resort. PHX is the
  home of American and Southwest also has a big
  operation here. This is one of the hubs of American
  Airlines (AA). Southwest also has a large presence
  here. The airport is served by many international
  carriers as well as U.S. domestic airlines.

73. Climb or visit the Seven Summits

I'm not a mountain climber. In Jamaica, our tallest mountain is the Blue Mountain range which peaks at 7,402'. I hiked it twice when I was a cadet in high school. It's actually a lot of fun. I don't really have any desire to hike or climb any more mountains, but I do love to look at them from a distance.

I've seen Mt. Fuji from the air, and it's magnificent. I was flying on ANA's 787 the second day of its operation and the first flight of that airplane. But alas, this is not one of the seven summits.

I've also seen Everest from Nagarkot in Nepal and Kilimanjaro from nearby Tanzania. And I've been to Denali National Park in Alaska. So, I've been closer than many, I guess, now that I think about it all.

There is something called the Seven Summits Challenge, the mountaineering challenge, pioneered by Richard Bass, the first person to climb all seven Summits. There's a great story about Bass here – www.latimes.com/local/obituaries/la-me-0730-richard-bass-20150730-story.html. Are you up for it?

Here are some more details about the Summits in
case you are so inclined to make this happen:

**Mount Aconcagua in Argentina [South
America]**

Your closest airport seems to be Mendoza,
Argentina (MDZ). You can't get there nonstop from
the U.S., but you can certainly fly into Buenos Aires,
Argentina (EZE), then take Aerolineas Argentinas
(AR) from EZE or the downtown airport (AEP). Or fly
into Santiago, Chile (SCL) and take Gol (G3).

Once in Mendoza, you'd have to arrange
transportation from local expedition companies that
specialize in getting climbers to the mountain.

Mount Carstensz in Papua, Indonesia [Asia]

It looks like the closest airport is in Timika,
Indonesia (TIM), about two hours away by car. Timika
is served by Garuda Indonesia (GA) from both
Denpasar Bali, Indonesia (DPS), and Jakarta,
Indonesia (CGK).

Mount Denali in Alaska, U.S. [North America]

Head to Anchorage, Alaska (ANC), then rent a car and drive up to Denali National Park. It's a beautiful drive up. Ensure you keep an eye out for large animals running across the road. I just missed a bear or a deer by inches on my last drive.

You may want to check on accommodations around the park before you go as it's quite sparse unless you are going camping before the hike up to the peak.

Mount Elbrus in Russia [Europe]

Mount Elbrus is the highest mountain in Europe. It is located in the south of Russia near the Georgia border. The nearest airport is Nalchik, Russia (NAL), with service from Istanbul (IST) on Onur Air (8Q) and from Moscow-Vnukovo (VKO) on UTair (UT). The Mineralnye Vody Airport (MRV) may also be used, but is about 200 kilometers from the mountain. All three Moscow airports (DME, SVO, VKO) offer air service, as does St. Petersburg, Russia (LED), and Dubai, United Arab Emirates (DXB), on FlyDubai (FZ). You do have to rent a car with a driver from the airports to make it to the town of Terksol, which is located at the base of the mountain. You can find additional information about Elbrus at www.elbrus.su/. It includes information on how to organize tours and climbs.

Mount Everest in Nepal [Asia]

This is the granddaddy of mountains. At 29,029' (8,848 meters), it's the world's tallest mountain. I have two friends who have made it to base camp. I'm so proud of them. It's quite expensive to do a climb, but you can certainly do base camp or head to towns that are close to it.

My keen interest in Everest is the fact that you first fly into Katmandu, Nepal (KTM), which, if you've not been there, is an amazing place to visit. Katmandu has quite a bit of lift so you won't have any issues getting there. You obtain your visa on arrival, so bring money with you. They also take a photo on arrival as well, and you also have to pay for that. Here are some airlines that serve KTM:

- Air China (CA) from Chengdu, People's Republic
  of China (CTU)
- Air India (AI) from Delhi (DEL) and Mumbai,
  India (BOM)
- Cathay Dragon (KA) from Hong Kong (HKG)
- Etihad (EY) from Abu Dhabi, United Arab
  Emirates (AUH)
- FlyDubai (FZ) from Dubai, United Arab Emirates
  (DXB)
- Malaysia Airlines (MH) from Kuala Lumpur,
  Malaysia (KUL)
- SilkAir (MI) from Singapore (SIN)
- Thai Airways (TG) from Bangkok-Suvarnabhumi,
  Thailand (BKK)
- Turkish Airlines (TK) from Istanbul, Turkey (IST)

Once in KTM, you fly to Lukla, Nepal (LUA), which
is one of the world's most dangerous airports due to its
approach and unforgiving terrain. Tara Air (TA), whose
parent company is Yeti Airlines, flies the route. You may
have to buy a ticket if your airline doesn't have an
agreement. Usually, most airlines don't have agreements
with airlines that small.

When I visited Nepal, I did not get a chance to log the
airport, but plan on doing so the next time I visit. I did do
a flight to nowhere though, and got a chance to see Everest
a little closer than most. So much fun...

Once in Lukla, you link up with your guide and start
your trek. You can find more information about Everest at
adventure.nationalgeographic.com/adventure/everest.

Mount Kilimanjaro in Tanzania [Africa]

The highest mountain on the continent of Africa,
Mount Kilimanjaro, rises to 5,895 meters (19,340') above
sea level. Three of my friends have made it to the summit,
so I'm super pumped for them. I've only seen it from the
plains near the airport in Kilimanjaro. It's a sight to see.
As I watched it, I could hear Maasai people making
clicking sounds as they gathered wood nearby. It was quite
surreal. I was standing on the side of the road that led to
Arusha on end and the Kilimanjaro airport on the other
end.

You can either fly into Nairobi, Kenya (NBO), or
Kilimanjaro, Tanzania (JRO), meet with your guide or
tour, and be on your way. You can find additional
information at www.tanzaniaparks.com/kili.html and

www.nationalgeographicexpeditions.com/expeditions/kili manjaro-climb/detail.

Nairobi is the home of Kenya Airways (KQ), which flies to many destinations in Europe and Africa, so you won't have any shortage of ways to get there. In Africa, there are usually tag flights that only go in one direction so watch out for those. As an example, Swiss flies from Zurich to Dar es Salaam, Tanzania, to Nairobi, Kenya, then back to Zurich. Here are some airlines that fly into Nairobi, Kenya (NBO):

- British Airways (BA) from London-Heathrow (LHR)
- Emirates (EK) from Dubai, United Arab Emirates (DXB)
- Etihad (EY) from Abu Dhabi, United Arab Emirates (AUH)
- Ethiopian Airlines (ET) from Addis Ababa, Ethiopia (ET)
- Kenya Airways (KQ) from African, Asian, European, and the Middle Eastern destinations
- KLM (KL) from Amsterdam (AMS)
- Lufthansa (LH) from Frankfurt, Germany (FRA)
- Swiss (LX) from Dar es Salaam, Tanzania (DAR)

- Qatar (QR) from Doha, Qatar (DOH)

  Here are some airlines that fly into Kilimanjaro, Tanzania (JRO):

  - Condor (DE) from Mombasa, Kenya (MBA) [you would join this flight in Frankfurt, Germany (FRA)]

  - Ethiopian Airlines (ET) from Addis Ababa, Ethiopia (ET)

  - KLM (KL) from Dar es Salaam, Tanzania (DAR) [you would join this flight in Amsterdam (AMS)]

  - Qatar Airways (QR) from Zanzibar, Tanzania (ZNZ) [you would join this flight in Doha, Qatar (DOH)]. There's also flight nonstop from Doha.

  - Turkish Airlines (TK) from Mombasa, Kenya (MBA) [you would join this flight in Istanbul (IST)]

Mount Vinson in Antarctica

You perhaps did not think there are mountains so tall in Antarctica, did you? Well, Mount Vinson is 16,050' (4,892 meters). You thought the others were difficult to get to? This one is even more difficult as it's about 660 nautical miles from the South Pole.

The closest I've been to that region is a trip to the
southern-most city in the world, Punta Arenas, Chile.
Now, before you say that's not the southernmost city,
there's a little more. Although Ushuaia, Argentina, is
more southern, it's actually not attached to the
continent, but on an island. Go check it out. I did not
make this up. I too wondered as you are now. When I
went to Punta Arenas, they actually have a certificate
that says, "The Southernmost City" ☺. But I'm
digressing.

I mention these cities as your voyage will perhaps
start in either of these cities Punta Arenas, Chile
(PUQ), or Ushuaia, Argentina (USH). You can take
Aerolineas Argentinas (AR) from Buenos Aires-Jorge
Newberry, Argentina (AEP), to USH and LATAM
from Santiago, Chile (SCL), to PUQ.

Aeromexico (AM), Air Canada (AC), Air France
(AF), Air New Zealand (NZ), air europa (UX), Alitalia
(AZ), American Airlines (AA), Copa Airlines (CM),
Cubana (CU), Delta Air Lines (DL), Emirates (EK),
GOL (G3), Iberia (IB), LATAM (LA), Lufthansa
(LH), Qatar (QR), SAS (SK), Turkish Airlines (TK)
and United (UA) all serve Buenos Aires-Ezezia (EZE).

You can take a shuttle bus or a taxi between the two Buenos Aires airports.

Aerolineas Argentinas (AR), Aeromexico (AM), Air Canada (AC), Air France (AF), Alitalia (AZ), American Airlines (AA), British Airways (BA), Copa Airlines (CM), Delta Air Lines (DL), GOL (G3), Iberia (IB), KLM (KL), LATAM (LA), Qantas (QF) and United (UA) all serve Santiago (SCL).

For U.S. citizens, a visa is not required for either Argentina or Chile. If you're a UK citizen, in Chile you pay the reciprocal visa fee on arrival, before you clear immigration.

You can find additional information about the climb at www.rmiguides.com/vinson-massif and http://7summits.com/vinson/vinson.htm.

74. Ride a camel

I'm not a fan of riding animals at all; but its
apparently a thing ☺. My only time was riding a camel
in Giza, Egypt, many years ago when I visited the
pyramids.

There are a few places around the world where
camels are the sole or the normal means of
transportation. Camels are not like horses and donkeys,
which use their tails efficiently. Camels basically just
sit there and do nothing while flies take over. Plus,
there is the smell. I'm just managing your expectations

So, if you want something different on your next
trip, then check these out these excursions:

- Take a camel tour through the western Sahara. You
  can find details at
  www.wildmorocco.com/trekking-morocco/sahara-
  desert-trekking/. Take Royal Air Maroc (AT) from
  New York-JFK to Casablanca (CMN) and then to
  Marrakech (RAK). Additional flights also
  available from Europe and the Middle East.

- Ride a camel over the sand dunes in Dubai, United
  Arab Emirates (DXB). Dubai is the home of

Emirates (EK) so you can get here from almost
everywhere in the world. Etihad (EY) flies into
Abu Dhabi (AUH) and from there you can take a
90-minutes shuttle bus to Dubai. At the moment,
there are no U.S. carriers serving Dubai, but you
can take Emirates from several cities or connect
over Europe via any of the European hubs. You
can find a few companies that offer these tours at
www.viator.com/Dubai/d828-ttd and
www.getyourguide.com/dubai-1173/camel-riding-
tours-tc178/.

- Take a camel ride near the pyramids of Giza in
  Egypt. Fly into Cairo, Egypt (CAI), then hire a car
  to get out to Giza. It's quite liberating to see the
  Great Pyramids from atop a camel.

- Take a camel ride in Marrakech, Morocco (RAK).
  You can fly in RAK on Royal Air Maroc (AT)
  from Casablanca (CMN). They fly to CMN
  nonstop from JFK. There is also service from all
  the major European airline hubs. Additional
  information at www.wildmorocco.com/.

75. Take a day trip to a North American City

There are many fine cities around the globe that
have frequent airline schedules, making it easy to have
a day trip. You get in first thing in the morning and
leave on the last flight of the day or the red-eye flight
if it's just after midnight. Here are a few options for
you:

Chicago [Midway (MDW), O'Hare (ORD)]

Fly into Midway and out of O'Hare or vice versa.
To get into the city, take the Chicago Transit Authority
(CTA) Blue Line from ORD or the Orange Line from
MDW. Buy a Venta card and charge it with about $10
or so if you intend on taking the trains a few times.
Once in the city, you can check out the following:

- Ride the red line and brown line "El" in Chicago
  and take in the skyline.
- See the John Hancock Center
  (http://www.johnhancockcenterchicago.com/) and
  head up to the Observatory to get a great view of
  the city of Chicago.

- Visit <u>Millennium Park</u> (<u>http://www.cityofchicago.org/city/en/depts/dca/supp_info/millennium_park.html</u>). Here, you can enjoy a concert as well as the Bean. This is a giant metallic bean, formally known as The Cloud Gate Sculpture, that shows your reflection.

- Climb (O.K. take the elevator) to the top of the <u>Willis Tower</u> (<u>http://www.willistower.com/</u>). (As an aside, there is also a <u>Willis Building</u> (<u>http://www.willis.com/about_willis/the_willis_building/</u>) in London.) From here, you get a view of the city as well.

- Go to Midway airport and listen to Frank Sinatra songs as you go from floor to floor in the parking garage.

New York City [Islip McArthur (ISP), New York-JFK, LaGuardia (LGA), Newark-Liberty (EWR), White Plains (HPN)]

New York is one of my favorite cities to visit. It's also a top visited city for people around the world as well. Actually, many people think it's the capital of the U.S. ☺, but it's not. Washington D.C. is the

capital. There's lots to do and see. Here are a few of
my favorite things:

- Eat pasta in Little Italy
  (http://www.littleitalynyc.com/) in New York.

- See the Statue of Liberty
  (http://www.nps.gov/stli/index.htm).

- Go to the 911 Memorial
  (http://www.911memorial.org/).

- Head to the top of the Empire State Building
  (http://www.esbnyc.com/) for a good view of the
  city.

- Visit Central Park
  (http://www.centralparknyc.org/).

- There are many museums to choose from; try the
  MOMA (http://www.moma.org/) or the
  Guggenheim (http://www.guggenheim.org/) for
  starters.

- Watch the Today Show (http://www.today.com/),
  or Good Morning America live.

- Take a walk down Broadway then go see a
  Broadway show (http://www.broadway.com/).
  You can get last minute tickets at the TKTS

http://www.tdf.org/TDF_ServicePage.aspx?id=56 booth.

- Visit Times Square.
- Check out the High Line which garden walkway that runs above the city streets in lower Manhattan. It actually follows old train tracks. http://www.thehighline.org/

Portland, Oregon (PDX)

- See the Spruce Goose, the large airplane that was built by Howard Hughes. You can find information at http://www.sprucegoose.org. This is located outside of the city, though, so it may be all you can do in a day trip.
- On a different weekend (or the same, if you wish), head to Houston (IAH, HOU) to see the tomb of Howard Hughes in the heart of the city. Details at http://www.death2ur.com/howard_hughes_gravesite.htm.
- Visit the Portland Saturday Market – Take the Tri Met Max Light Rail (http://trimet.org/max/) Red Line towards downtown and get off at the Skidmore Fountain stop for the Portland Saturday

Market (on Sundays Too). You can find details at
http://www.portlandsaturdaymarket.com/.

San Francisco [Oakland (OAK), San Francisco (SFO), San Jose (SJO)]

- Walk across the Golden Gate Bridge

- Head for Sausalito by car. This city sits across the bay and is worth seeing. Make sure you get some ice cream.

- Hike the Muir Wood Forest and marvel at the tall redwood trees. You will need a car.

- Party in the South of Market area. This is in the downtown part of San Francisco, typically between 7th and 12th Streets on Folsom Street. There are a number of clubs in this area.

- Take a cable car ride. This is essential when you visit San Francisco. Start at the city center and go all the way to the end of the line at Fisherman's Wharf.

- Visit the Cable Car Museum.

- Go to Fisherman's Wharf and see the sea lions hanging around as well as the many street performers.

- Tour Alcatraz. Ensure that you purchase tickets beforehand as usually they are sold out on day of.

Seattle (SEA)

- Visit Pike's Market and watch the fish mongers throw fish. Additional information is at http://www.pikeplacemarket.org/.
- See the Space Needle.
- Hang out in Capitol Hill.
- See the city's underground.
- Go bar hopping in the downtown area.
- Watch planes at Boeing Field.
- Tour the Museum of Flight.
- Visit the British Airways Concorde on static display.
- Visit the Boeing Factory at Paine Field (PAE) in Everett, Washington.

Toronto (YYZ)

- Take a drive down to Niagara Falls.
- See the CN Tower.
- Take a bike tour of the city.
- Take a craft beer tour.

- Visit Toronto Island and tour by bike.

- Visit the Ontario Wine Country.

- Take the 501 Trolley down Queen Street.

76. Visit upwards of three countries all during the same day

There are a few ways to do this. It's more of seeing how many countries you can connect in rather than "visiting" ☺. A good one used to be flying from Cairns, Australia (CNS), to Guam (GUM), then to Honolulu (HNL) on United Airlines (UA), but that airline no longer serves CNS. Here are a few others you could try:

• Leave any European city on the first flight of the day and connect in either Amsterdam, Frankfurt, London, Paris, Rome, Milan, or Vienna, then take a flight to Canada and then a same-day connecting flight to the U.S. If you do the schedules right, you may be able to get another country in before the day is over.

• Leave any European city on the first flight of the day and connect in either Amsterdam (AMS), Frankfurt (FRA), London (LHR/LGW), Paris (CDG), Rome (FCO), Milan (MXP), or Vienna (VIE), take a flight to Canada and then a same-day

connecting flight to the U.S., and then onto another
country, typically Mexico, the Caribbean, or
Central America.

- Start your day in Auckland, New Zealand (AKL)
  then fly to Sydney, Australia (SYD), and get a
  flight to any other country from there.

77. Be in two continents in less than 10 minutes

This one is really cool; just hop on a flight to Istanbul (IST). If your local airline does not serve Istanbul, check your pass bureau for pass agreements with other airlines that do. Turkish Airlines (TK) is the home airline in Istanbul.

If you are in the U.S., you can take Turkish Airlines (TK) nonstop from various U.S. cities or fly to any of the Europe and Middle Eastern hubs and then fly to Istanbul.

Istanbul is in the continent of Asia and Europe. Just a bridge separates the two continents.

There is a ferry that you take between the two continents. The view is breathtaking as you traverse the river.

78. Go shopping in a foreign country

I'm not a big fan of shopping, but I know many of
you are. For me, I know exactly what I want and where
to get it. I go there, get it and I'm out of there. But,
thankfully, we are all not the same.

Since we can fly to other countries, we can make
use of the great shopping deals worldwide due to the
value of the US dollar. Here are a few places with
great shopping around the world:

- **14th Street area in New York**. There are many
  different places to shop in New York; this area is
  just one of them. New York is accessible by five
  airports, Islip (ISP), JFK, La Guardia (LGA),
  Newark-Liberty (EWR), and, although a little
  farther way, White Plains (HPN). There is of
  course no shortage of airlines serving the New
  York area. From these airports, you can get public
  transportation into New York City, then take the #s
  1, 2 or 3 to the 14th Street Station. You can read
  about other shopping areas in New York from
  Frommers at
  http://www.frommers.com/destinations/new-york-
  city/663769.

- **JJ Market (Chatuchak) in Bangkok.** This market
  is huge (about 35 acres)! Plus, it has some fantastic
  deals, and you can buy almost anything. It is a
  weekend market, and it's best you get there very
  early in the morning for the best deals and less
  crowds. The closest subway is the BTS station Mo
  Chit, which you can access from the city center.
  Bangkok is served by two airports Don Mueang
  (DMK) and Suvarnabhumi (BKK). You can take a
  train into the city center from both airports, then
  take the BTS to the market. You have a wide
  choice of airlines here, including the home airlines
  Thai Airways (TG) into BKK and Air Asia,
  Bangkok Airways (PG), Nok Air (DD), and Thai
  Asia Airways (FD).

- **Orchard Road in Singapore.** Singapore is home
  to Singapore Airlines (SQ), Scoot (TZ), and Silkair
  (MI). This is the main shopping street in
  Singapore. The stores range from high fashion to
  shopping malls to mom and pops. It's also a very
  beautiful area to walk as well.

- **Haggle at the markets in Beijing (PEK).** These
markets are all over the city. You can find a list of
some of them at
http://www.chinahighlights.com/beijing/article-
best-shopping-areas.htm. But all you have to do
when you get there is look around or ask your hotel
concierge for assistance.

- **The Mall of America in Minneapolis (MSP).** The
mall is located very close to the airport, and it has
everything you'll ever need. It's also like no other
mall you've ever visited. From the airport, take the
light rail to the mall. You can find additional
information about the mall at
https://www.mallofamerica.com/.

- **Oxford Street and Camden Market in London.**
Ah London. Like New York, there are tons of
places to shop. Oxford Street is one of the busiest
with many shops, and the famous Oxford Circus is
at its center. Actually, that's your Tube stop on the
Bakerloo, Central, and Victoria Lines. Camden
Market is the opposite of Oxford Street, and that's
why it's famous. You can find all kinds of things

there, and it also has a food market that has
extremely good ethnic foods. Also, the people
watching is divine. The Tube stop of this one is
Camden Town on the Northern Line. You can find
more information on the market at
http://www.camden-market.org/. Of course getting
to London, you have many flight options as well as
airport options. The closest is London City (LCY
in the heart of the city as well as Gatwick (LGW),
Heathrow (LHR), Luton (LTN), Stansted (STN),
and, a little further away, Southend (SEN).

- **Stanley Market in Hong Kong (HKG)**. My first
time here was actually really cool. I went with a
Hong Kong native, and he took me around and
showed me which items were designer items and
which were fakes. You'll get really good authentic
designer items here that did not make the final cut
when the buyers inspected them. Things that have
a flaw, such as a bad stitch or a color that is not
right, are rejected. Instead of tossing them away,
those products end up as great deals at Stanley
Market. Here are instructions on how to get there

once you arrive in Hong Kong – http://www.hk-stanley-market.com/getting-there.htm.

- **The West Edmonton Mall in Edmonton, Alberta, Canada (YEG).** This is the largest mall in North America. Yes, as large at the Mall of America is, this one is larger. Actually, I think the Mall of America was modeled after this one. You fly into Edmonton (YEG), which is served by Air Canada (AC), Air North (4N), Air Transat (TS), Alaska (AS), American (AA), Central Mountain Air (9N), Delta (DL), First Air (7F) Icelandair (FI), KLM (KL), Sunwing (WG), United (UA), and WestJet (WS). Either rent a car for the 25-minute drive, or take a combination of two buses for a commute of a little over an hour.

79. Take a swamp boat tour in Louisiana

The state of Louisiana in the southern U.S. has many bayous and swamps. All kinds of animals live in these swamps, including alligators. A few tour companies aim to give you a taste of the swamps. A few years ago, my office had a retreat in New Orleans, and I was able to do a tour. It is quite amazing.

Check out the Jean Lafitte Swamp and Airboat Tours to get a taste of what I'm talking about. Find details at www.jeanlafitteswamptour.com/.

New Orleans, LA (MSY) is the closest airport, and that is served by Air Canada (AC), Air Transat (TS), Alaska (AS), American (AA), Delta (DL), Frontier (F9), JetBlue (B6), Southwest (WN), Spirit (NK), and United (UA).

Baton Rouge (BTR) and Lafayette, LA (LFT) are alternate airports. You could just rent a car to complete the journey.

80. Go to the rodeo

Rodeo is big business. As a kid growing up in
Jamaica, each year there was a livestock show called
Denbigh Agricultural Show named after the place it
was held. I enjoyed going there, and, as a young child
with my parents, it just seemed so large. I learned so
much about agriculture and farming. It showcased the
different foods from around the country, so it was
intriguing to see which item came from which parts of
the country.

That event is now in its 65th year (2017) and still
going. Find details at www.jas.gov.jm/Denbigh.html if
you ever get to Jamaica when it's being held, typically
the end of July to the beginning of August. You can fly
into Kingston (KIN) or Montego Bay (MBJ), rent a
car, and head out to Denbigh in Clarendon.

You would think that, living in Houston that has a
rodeo each year, I'd attend. But not so. I've never been
to the rodeo in Houston. I've been to the barbecue
cook-off, of which Continental, now United Airlines,
is a sponsor, and that is a lot of fun. Here in Houston,
the trail riders, including horseback riders and chuck
wagons, all come into town like it's the olden days.

It's a sight to see, really. The Houston Live Stock
Show and Rodeo is usually held for three weeks
starting about the second week of March.

It features livestock demonstrations, competitions,
and concerts as well as the barbecue cook-off I
mentioned earlier. You can find more details at
www.rodeohouston.com/.

Houston is one of the hubs for United (UA) and
has two airports, Intercontinental (IAH) and Hobby
(HOU). All the U.S.-based airlines serve the city
except Allegiant. And, due to United's international
network, you can get here from anywhere in the world.

Calgary, Alberta, Canada (YEG), holds the
Calgary Stampede. Calgary is the home of WestJet
(WS). The stampede is usually held in July for a little
under two weeks, starting the second week. You can
find additional information at
www.calgarystampede.com/stampede.

I've not been to this event as yet, but want to check
it out at some point. And you should too, and let me
know what you think and how it went.

81. Go see a theatre production in a foreign country or city

I've always loved the theatre; not sure why I never took up acting, but I'm digressing. When I was in college in New York, I did a course called The New York Theatre Experience. I loved it as we had a chance to see about five Broadway shows, including the musical *Legs Diamond*, which only ran for a month and a half. I also had a chance to go backstage to see how it's all done. It's fascinating, I'll tell you.

Also, growing up in Jamaica, we had pantomime, which was held at the Ward Theatre in downtown Kingston. I don't think I missed any of the performances while growing up.

As such, when I travel I sometimes try to see a play. I saw *Mama Mia* and *Les Miserables* in London, or was that in New York for *Les Miserables*? Umm… Anyway, you get where I'm going with this one.

Just go watch a show when you visit a foreign country. Here are just a few options for you:

- **London (LCY, LGW, LHR, LTB, SEN, STN).**
  You can get good last-minute tickets from the

TKTS booth in Leicester Square, or you can go to the theatre that is showing your play and check for last-minute discount tickets. Leicester Square is in the heart of the London Theatre District. Go here for more details – http://www.tkts.co.uk/.

- **New York (EWR, HPN, ISP, JFK, LGA, SWF).** The same is true here, there is a TKTS booth in Times Square, or you can go to the theatre that is showing your play and check for last-minute discount tickets.

In New York, there are some very good Off Broadway and Off Off Broadway plays. It's not that these theatres are not on Broadway physically, although some aren't, but that the number of seats a theatre has determines its classification. As the theatres are smaller, you enjoy the performance much more and feel like a part of the production. And oftentimes, the actors just sit on the stage and answer questions after the show, which is pretty sweet. Head over to https://www.tdf.org/ for more details.

- **Sydney (SYD)**. You've seen the iconic Sydney Opera House in many photos. How about going to see an Opera performance there the next time you are in town? More details are available at http://www.sydneyoperahouse.com/.

- **Milan (MXP).** On the subject of iconic opera houses, why not check out a performance at the 200-year-old Teatro alla Scala, better known simply as "La Scala," where you can also catch a ballet or symphony? You can find more details at http://www.teatroallascala.org/en/index.html.

- **Toronto (YYZ, YTZ).** Check out a performance of the Toronto Symphony Orchestra. Head over to https://www.tso.ca/ for details.

- **Vienna (VIE)**. Grab a ticket for the Vienna Philharmonic Orchestra. Check out this site for tickets and details – http://www.wienerphilharmoniker.at/en.

And, if you are ever in Jamaica, go see a pantomime or a stage play in the capital city of Kingston.

82. Go skiing somewhere cool

I'm not a skier. The closest I came to skiing was
doing an hour of snowboarding lessons in
Montrose/Telluride many years ago. But I know that
many of you are. As an airline employee, it's great to
get out there and live with passion, as Tony Robbins
says. So why not go out and enjoy what you do best?
And, if you are a skier, there are many places
worldwide just waiting for you to zip down the slopes.

Here are a just a few to consider:

- Chile (SCL) – Chile is one of those countries that
  have deserts, mountains (the Andes), snow, and the
  ocean. Amazing, huh? So you can go skiing there
  as well. There is a list of resorts at
  www.powderhounds.com/SouthAmerica/Chile/Bes
  t-Ski-Resorts.aspx. The closest major international
  airport to the slopes is Santiago, Chile (SCL),
  which is served by many of the major worldwide
  carriers, so getting down there is not an issue.
  LATAM (LA) is the home carrier. Remember, it's
  in the southern hemisphere, so you'll be skiing in
  the June/July/August timeframe. Once in Santiago,
  you can arrange local transportation, including

taking buses to the resorts. Check out this site for
additional information
www.santiagotourist.com/chilean-bus-travel/.
Depending on the resort you are visiting, you can
then fly into a closer airport.

- **Dubai, United Arab Emirates (DXB)** –
Everything is bigger in Dubai and also man-made.
Well, not everything ☺. But it's the desert, so
obviously this ski area is man-made. Yup, you can
go skiing in the desert. They've created an indoor
ski slope called Ski Dubai in the Mall of the
Emirates, and it looks just as good as any complete
with the cold temperatures. The Mall of Emirates is
a stop on the Dubai Metro. Check out
www.theplaymania.com/skidubai for details.

- **Europe** – As there are so many places to ski in
Europe, I found this article that talks about the 10
best places to go. Check it out at
www.outsideonline.com/1927841/top-10-ski-
resorts-europe

- **Montrose/Telluride, CO (MTJ)** – Fly into the
main airport here and then take any of the multiple

transportation to get to the resorts. Check here for
details – www.tellurideskiresort.com.

- **New Zealand (AKL, CHC)** – You may not think
  about New Zealand as a place to ski, but it is. Since
  it is in the southern hemisphere, this is another
  place where you can ski in the June/July/August
  timeframe. Check details at
  www.newzealandski.co.nz.

- **South Africa (JNB)** – You perhaps don't think
  about South Africa when you think about skiing,
  but you can. One of the resorts is Tiffindell. Go to
  www.tiffindell.co.za/. Remember that the seasons
  are flipped as South Africa is in the Southern
  Hemisphere, so you'll be skiing in
  June/July/August ☺. You can fly into
  Johannesburg, fly to Umtata (UTT) on South
  African Airways, rent a car, and drive to the resort.
  It's not exactly the easiest place to get to, but they
  have directions at
  www.tiffindell.co.za/getting_here and of course
  you can use your online mapping software.

- **Vail, CO (EGE)** – Check out www.vail.com.
  Check flight loads as sometimes the flights may be
  weight-restricted. You will need a car, or you can
  take paid transportation from the airport to your
  resort.

- **Vermont (BTV)** – Another great place to ski is the
  slopes of Vermont in the Northeastern U.S. Lots of
  information is available at www.skivermont.com/.
  You fly into Burlington, Vermont (BTV), and then
  either rent a car or take the local transports to more
  than 40 resorts in the state.

83. Fly to the Memphis airport (MEM) just to get barbecue

Although MEM is no longer the hub it used to be since the merger of Northwest Airlines with Delta and the subsequent de-hubbing of the airport, the barbecue in the airport is some of the best around.

The lines are usually very long, so plan your flights accordingly; you should be able to do it on a quick turn though. The lines may not be too long nowadays with reduced air service. There are usually several other airline employees in the line picking up some grub. If you are running late, good luck with trying to move your way up in line.

The name of the place is Interstate Bar-B-Que. It's closed on Saturdays but open 12 hours a day from 7:30a the rest of the week. It's located in Concourse B.

84. Spend some time at an aviation museum

Our industry has a lot of history. Start at these sites
www.aviationmuseum.eu and
http://www.airplaneexhibits.com/list-of-air-museums-
exhibits-airparks.htm. Here are a few suggestions for
museums to visit:

Berlin, Germany (TXL, SXF)

Deutsches Technikmuseum Berlin
(http://www.sdtb.de/) – This museum is bigger than it
looks from the outside and will take you about three
hours or so to walk through. There is even a train
exhibit in the back that I guarantee you will love. You
can even get to walk through some of the trains. The
museum is accessible by train, bus, or car although I
recommend the train as it's a short walk from the
station.

Edinburgh, Scotland (EDI)

The National Museum of Flight
(http://www.nms.ac.uk/our_museums/museum_of_flig
ht.aspx), a division of the National Museums of
Scotland, is worth a visit, especially since G-BOAA, a

retired British Airways Concorde, is located there. The
museum is located in a town called East Fortune. You
can find more details on accessing it at
http://www.edinburgh.org/pass/attractions/museum-of-flight. The address is: East Fortune Airfield, East
Lothian, EH39 5LF.

Houston, Texas (HOU, IAH)

1940 Air Museum at Houston Hobby Airport
(http://www.1940airterminal.org/) – This gem sits
hidden at the other end of Houston-Hobby Airport
(HOU). You do have to get a car to get there, or you
can take a local bus from the Hobby Airport and walk
the rest of the way. You can also walk from Hobby
Airport, but it will take a while as you are walking
around the perimeter of the airport. Which is not too
bad as you can watch some landings as you do, but it is
quite a way to walk.

Once there, it's as if you've stepped into 1940
again. The curators are very friendly and happy to see
other airline enthusiasts. Unfortunately, you cannot
make it up to the tower at the moment as they are
doing repairs, but you can sit on the benches outside

and watch the airport operations. If you love airline
memorabilia, this terminal is full of it. Of course, since
it's in Houston, the memorabilia are mostly from
Continental Airlines and its merged airlines. It's all so
fun to see what aviation was like back then.

London, England (LCY, LGW, LHR, LTN, SEN, STN)

The Imperial War Museum in Duxford, England –
http://duxford.iwm.org.uk. I recommend that you
schedule your visit around a time when they have an
airshow, if at all possible. You can see the airshow
schedule at
http://duxford.iwm.org.uk/server/show/nav.00d004. It
is then necessary to rent a car to get there. You can
find a map with directions on their Web site or use
Google Maps.

New York, New York (EWR, HPN, ISP, JFK, LGA, SWF)

The Intrepid Sea, Air & Space Museum
(http://www.intrepidmuseum.org/) in New York
Harbor is home to yet another Concorde (G-BOAD) as
well as one of the space shuttles, *Enterprise*. The

museum sits on the west side of Manhattan at Pier 86,
12th Ave. and 46th Street, on an aircraft carrier, the
Intrepid; which is the aircraft carrier moored at the
docks. You can reach it by car or take the NYC
subway and walk over to site. The closest subway stop
is 50th St. and 8th Ave on the C and E lines. Check
opening times at http://www.intrepidmuseum.org/Plan-
Your-Visit.aspx. And remember you can save by
booking online before you go.

Paris, France (BVA, CDG, ORY)

The Musée de l'air et de l'espace
(http://www.museeairespace.fr/) LeBourget, Paris –
For this one, you fly into Paris-Charles de Gaulle,
Paris-Orly or Paris-Beauvais and head for Le Bourget
at the station with the same name via the RER B
subway line. Once there, take the local bus that says
Le Bourget and get off just outside the museum. Or
you can plan on visiting during the Paris Airshow,
which is held every other year. There is actually a
plaque that commemorates the place Charles
Lindbergh landed. It's out on the taxiways; look for it.

Portland, Oregon (PDX)

The **Evergreen Aviation & Space Museum**
(http://www.evergreenmuseum.org/) is home of the
Spruce Goose. For this one, you need a car as you have
to fly into Portland, Oregon (PDX), and then head
south to the small town of McMinnville, Oregon. If
nothing else, you will have a nice drive down there.
Try not to get distracted by the many vineyards in the
area though. As a matter of fact, the museum itself sits
on a vineyard.

San Diego, California (SAN)

The U.S.S. Midway Museum
(http://www.midway.org/) – Like the Intrepid
museum, this one is located on a battle ship. Fly into
San Diego's Lindbergh Field, which is also a museum
in its own right. As you fly into SAN, if you look on
the left side of the plane, you can see the ship, located
at the San Diego waterfront (910 N Harbor Dr., San
Diego, CA 92101). This floating museum is easily
accessed from the airport via the bus (992) heading
downtown. If you feel up to it, you can take the walk
from the airport as well.

Seattle, Washington (SEA)

The Museum of Flight in Seattle, Washington – **www.museumofflight.org**, here you will get a chance to see one of the British Airways Concorde; actually, this is the one in which I've flown (G-BOAG). You fly into Seattle-Tacoma (SEA), and then you can take a bus, rent a car, or take a cab to the museum. Be sure to visit the terminal for Kings County Municipal airport that is across the other side of the runway. If you are lucky you may see a few unpainted Boeing 737s land as they come from Boeing's Renton, Washington, facility where they are made. You may also witness a delivery flight from one of the airlines.

Washington, D.C. Area (BWI, DCA, IAD)

The **Smithsonian National Air and Space Museum** (http://airandspace.si.edu/) in Washington, D.C. – Located in the capital city of the U.S., you can fly into Washington-Dulles (IAD), Washington-Reagan National (DCA), or Baltimore-Washington (BWI) airports. The Smithsonian holds the largest collection of historic airplanes and spacecraft in the world. The museum has two facilities: one near

Washington-Dulles and the other in the heart of the

city near the Washington Mall. The latter is accessible

by the D.C. Metro while the other is accessible by car.

85. See how many airports you can land at or take off from for one 24-hour period

This will take some planning, but I am sure you can put an itinerary together. Use the schedule program at www.passrider.com to help you. Remember to take red-eye flights so you won't need a hotel.

If you are in the U.S., you could work your way up the west coast starting in San Diego, then take a red-eye flight from say Seattle to the East Coast, then work your way back to the West Coast. Use the airlines' hubs to your advantage and use your agreements so you can fly multiple airlines. Here's a possible itinerary:

SAN-SEA-EWR-IAD-ATL-IAH-SFO-LAX-SAN.

In Europe, you can start in Ireland and end up in, say, Romania.

It used to be so much easier to do this as the passes were cheaper and there were more airlines. But its still doable.

86. Visit all of the states/provinces/counties in your country by air

This will take you a while to accomplish, but set a goal for yourself. The key here is that it is inexpensive as you work for an airline.

First make a list of all the airports in your region in a spreadsheet, then plan it out a little bit, and get started.

Take Canada for example. You could do all the provinces. Not as easy as it seems though, as it's difficult to get to some of the northern ones. You will need to take the likes of FirstAir (7F) to access some of these provinces. It is a fun airline, though, and the region is very beautiful.

For the U.S. states, this will take you a while. You can't fly from every state to the next, so you may have to do some backtracking to the airlines' hubs, which makes it fun anyways.

Start with the popular places as they will be easier.

87. Visit all the countries in any one continent

Not as bad as you think, but tricky; North America
is the easiest one of them all followed by South
America, although it will be interesting to get to
French Guiana (On Air France (AF) from Fort de
France, Martinique (FDF), or from Paris-Orly (ORY)),
Guyana (from Port of Spain, Trinidad on Caribbean
Airlines (BW) and New York on Delta Air Lines
(DL)), and Suriname (from Amsterdam as well as
French Guiana) as they have limited air service and
only from select cities, but it is doable.

Africa and Europe will take a while, and Antarctica
will be a challenge. Asia is pretty easy, although some
places are quite tricky. Just be systematic.

Good luck.

88. Visit every country in the world

You must think I am nuts by now, but I bet that you can already name four or five countries that you've visited in your lifetime. Just keep racking them up as time goes along.

Remember, if you connect via a country, it still counts. Each time you land and take off from an airport that has commercial air service, it counts. At the time of this writing, I have been to 121 countries and geographical territories. You can get a full list and all the rules from The Travelers' Century Club (http://travelerscenturyclub.org/).

89. Visit all the commercial airports in the world or at least in your immediate region, say your own country, state, etc.

Yes, this is a very lofty goal, but you just need to start at some point. Start with the state, province, or country where you live and work your way outwards. If any city has more than one airport, each time you fly to or from that city, fly from a different airport, if at all possible.

Here are some examples of cities with multiple commercial airports:

- Belfast, Northern Ireland (BFS): Belfast-International (BFS) and Belfast-City (BHD)
- Berlin (BER): Tegel (TXL), Schönefeld (SXF)
- Castries, St. Lucia: George F.L. Charles (SLU) and Hewanorra International (UVF)
- Chicago (CHI): Gary (GYY), Midway (MDW), and O'Hare (ORD)
- Dallas (DAL): Dallas/Fort Worth (DFW) and Love Field (DAL)
- Houston (HOU): Hobby (HOU) and Intercontinental (IAH)

- London (LON): Gatwick (LGW), Heathrow (LHR), London City (LCY), Luton (LTN), Southend (SEN), and Stansted (STN)
- Los Angeles (LAX): Burbank (BUR), Long Beach (LGB), Los Angeles (LAX), Ontario (ONT), and Orange County (SNA)
- Medellin, Colombia: Olaya Herrera Airport (EOH) and José María Córdova International Airport (MDE)
- Miami: Fort Lauderdale (FLL), Miami (MIA), Palm Beach (PBI)
- New York (NYC): Islip McArthur (ISP), John F. Kennedy (JFK), LaGuardia (LGA), Newark Liberty (EWR), Stewart/Newburg (SWF) and White Plains (HPN)
- Milan (MIL): Linate (LIN), Malpensa (MXP), Orio Al Serio (BGY), and Parma (PMF)
- Orlando, Florida (ORL): Orlando (MCO) and Sanford (SFB)
- Paris (PAR): Beauvais (BVA), Charles de Gaulle (CDG), and Orly (ORY)

- Reykjavik, Iceland (REK): Domestic (RKV) and
  Keflavik (KEF)

- Rio de Janeiro (RIO): Rio de Janeiro (GIG) and
  Santos Dumont (SDU)

- Rome (ROM): Ciampino (CIA) and Fiumicino
  (FCO)

- San Francisco (SFO): International (SFO),
  Oakland (OAK), and San Jose (SJC)

- São Paulo (SAO): Congonhas (CGH) and
  Guarulhos (GRU)

- Washington (WAS): Baltimore (BWI), Dulles
  (IAD), Reagan National (DCA).

Two Bonus Things

90. Fly all the different commercial aircraft types in existence

You can easily start with the larger companies Airbus (www.airbus.com) and Boeing (www.boeing.com) and work your way through the regional jets primarily by Bombardier and Embraer. When you fly look at the flight schedules and chose the open flights you want based on the aircraft type.

You may have to be creative to find select types that are still operating. I have airline friends who've flown all over the world, just to get on a unique aircraft type. You too can do the same. It makes great conversation at a cocktail party too.

Here are the popular Airbus, Boeing, Bombardier, Embraer, Fokker and McDonnell Douglas types:

a. Airbus Industries

    i.   300-600 (AB6)

    ii. 310 (310)

    iii. 318 (318)

    iv. 319-100 (319)

    v. 319-200 (319)

    vi. 319 neo

      vii. 320-200 (320)

     viii. 320 neo

      ix. 321-200 (321)

       x. 321 neo

      xi. 330-200 (332)

     xii. 330-300 (333)

    xiii. 330-800neo

    xiv. 330-900neo

     xv. 340-200 (340)

    xvi. 340-300 (343)

   xvii. 340-500 (345)

  xviii. 340-600 (346)

    xix. 350-900 (359)

     xx. 350-1000 (351)

    xxi. 380-800 (388)

  b. Boeing Company

       i. 727-100 (721)

      ii. 727-200 (722)

     iii. 737-200 (732)

     iv. 737-300 (733)

      v. 737-400 (734)

     vi. 737-500 (735)

    vii. 737-600 (736)

viii. 737-700 (73G)

ix. 737-800 (738)

x. 737-800 w/winglets (73H)

xi. 737 MAX 7 (7M7)

xii. 737 MAX 8 (7M8)

xiii. 737 MAX 9 (7M9)

xiv. 737 MAX 10 (7MJ)

xv. 737-900 (739)

xvi. 737-900ER (739)

xvii. 747-200 (742)

xviii. 747-300 (743)

xix. 747-300 Combi

xx. 747-400 (744)

xxi. 747-400 Combi (74M)

xxii. 747-8i (748)

xxiii. 757-200 (752)

xxiv. 757-300 (753)

xxv. 767-200 (762)

xxvi. 767-300 (763)

xxvii. 767-300ER (763)

xxviii. 767-400ER (764)

xxix. 777-200 (777)

xxx. 777-200ER (772)

      xxxi. 777-200LR (77L)

      xxxii. 777-300 (773)

      xxxiii. 777-300IGW (77W)

      xxxiv. 787-8 (788)

      xxxv. 787-9 (789)

      xxxvi. 787-10

  c. Bombardier

      i. CRJ-100 (CR1)

      ii. CRJ-200 (CR2)

      iii. CRJ-700 (CR7)

      iv. CRJ-900 (CR9)

  d. Embraer

      i. EMB-120 Brasilia (EM2)

      ii. ERJ-135 (ER3, SRJ)

      iii. ERJ-145 (ER4, ERJ

      iv. ERJ-170 (170)

      v. ERJ-175 (175)

      vi. ERJ-190 (190)

  e. Fairchild

      i. Dornier 328JET (FRJ)

  f. Fokker

      i. Fokker F28

      ii. Fokker 50, Fokker 70

    g. Lockheed

        i. L-1011 Tristar (L10)

       ii. L-1011 500 Tristar (L15)

    h. McDonnell Douglas

        i. DC-10 (D10)

       ii. MD-11 (M11)

      iii. MD-80 (M80)

91. Fly all the different airlines in the world

O.K., at least attempt it.

I've flown about 171 airlines now, and, of course, I want to fly them all or as many as I can. When you fly another airline, you get to experience a little of that airline's culture. If the airline is based in a different area other than where you live, you also experience the culture of that region.

Start by looking at your airline's pass agreements. When you have to go somewhere, see if you can fly on a new airline each time, even if your own airline flies there. If you do not have a pass agreement, ask your pass office if it is O.K. to write a letter to that airline and see if they will send you a pass. If you have to travel on company business, consider traveling on an airline other than your own; sometimes you don't have a choice anyways. If all else fails, you can plan ahead a little and buy a ticket, if it is not too costly. Make a list and check it off as you go.

Thanks for purchasing and reading this book! By now you should have all the necessary tools to maximize your travel benefits.

Head over to http://www.passrider.com/89things-thank-you so we can keep in touch and share even more travel advice. Sign up for my newsletter and you'll get periodic advice on maximizing your travel benefits even more. I can't wait to share more tips with you!

http://www.passrider.com/89things-thank-you.